PORT ARTHUR:
A Place of Misery

PORT ARTHUR:
A Place of Misery

Maggie Weidenhofer

MELBOURNE

Oxford University Press

OXFORD   AUCKLAND   NEW YORK

Oxford University Press, Walton Street, Oxford OX2 6DP

London Glasgow New York Toronto
Delhi Bombay Calcutta Madras Karachi
Kuala Lumpur Singapore Hong Kong Tokyo
Nairobi Dar es Salaam Cape Town
Melbourne Auckland

and associate companies in
Beirut Berlin Ibadan Mexico City

©Maggie Weidenhofer 1981
First published 1981

Designed by Derrick I. Stone

Weidenhofer, Maggie, 1941—.
  Port Arthur: A Place of Misery.

  Bibliography.
  Includes index.
  ISBN 0 19 554323 8
  1. Port Arthur (Tas.)—History.
  2. Penal Colonies, British—History. I Title.
  994.6′4

Printed at Griffin Press Limited, Netley, South Australia

For Bridget

Endpapers
A vignette of Port Arthur in about 1845 from above a large map of Tasman Peninsula. The shallow part of the bay has not yet been reclaimed.

Title page
A pair of leg-irons weighing about 5 kilograms. A chain often extended from the ankle chain up to the waist.

Contents

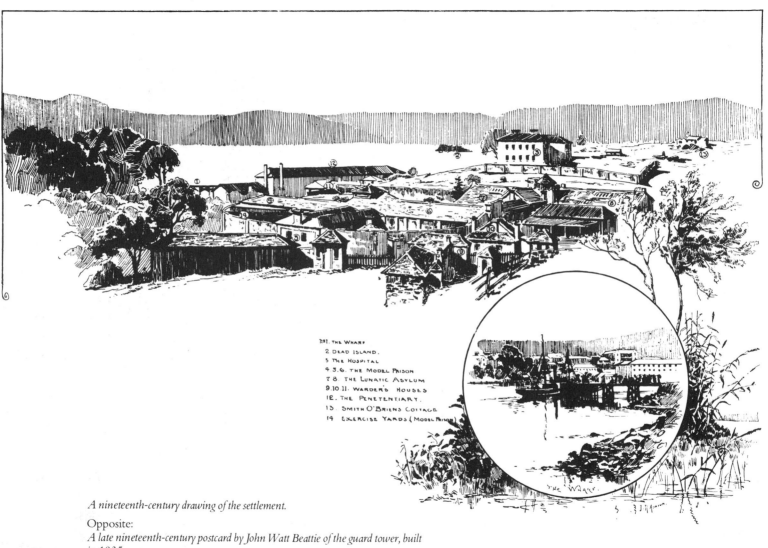

N°1. THE WHARF
2 DEAD ISLAND.
3 THE HOSPITAL
4 5 6. THE MODEL PRISON
7 8. THE LUNATIC ASYLUM
9 10 11. WARDER'S HOUSES
12. THE PENETENTIARY.
13. SMITH O'BRIENS COTTAGE
14 EXERCISE YARDS (MODEL PRISON)

THE WHARF

A nineteenth-century drawing of the settlement.

Opposite:
*A late nineteenth-century postcard by John Watt Beattie of the guard tower, built
in 1835.*

Foreword

Port Arthur represents a most significant period of Tasmania's history in so far as European settlement is concerned. It is a place associated not only with the colonization of Tasmania but Australia as a whole.

Maggie Weidenhofer has chosen a most appropriate title for this book, *Port Arthur: A Place of Misery*, for those who visit the area's tranquil and pleasant surrounds today cannot imagine the feelings and tribulations experienced by the earlier inhabitants of the last century. These are most vividly and sympathetically portrayed in this book, which has been thoroughly and well researched.

It is perhaps a tribute to gaoler and convict alike that they were able to survive and even prosper in what was such an isolated and foreign environment. It is a story of resilience and resourcefulness and not without touches of humour.

This book is easy to read and must prove invaluable not only to historians but also to tourists and others who wish to know more of Port Arthur, now an historic site, administered by the Tasmanian National Parks and Wildlife Service.

I wish it well.

Peter Murrell,
Director,
National Parks and Wildlife Service,
Tasmania

Preface

This book has grown from my curiosity about colonial days in Tasmania, transportees to the colony, their treatment as convicts and their lives as ex-convicts. Naturally, this curiosity encompassed the history of Port Arthur penal settlement and, after 1877, the emerging tourist industry there and the residents of the town. A book well supported with illustrations seemed to be needed—one which would satisfy the interest of the visitors who are intrigued by Port Arthur's past, as I am, as well as those people whose lives are entwined with its past and future.

Several Tasman Peninsula residents—Lorna Smith, Athol Wellard and the Senior Ranger at Port Arthur, Dick Mifsud—have assisted generously with answers to my questions. As well, for their assistance and for permission to reproduce documents and illustrations, my thanks are due to the State Library of New South Wales, including the Dixson and Mitchell libraries; the National Parks and Wildlife Service; the Public Record Office, London; the Queen Victoria Museum and Art Gallery, Launceston; the State Library of Tasmania, including the Allport Library and Museum of Fine Art and the W. L. Crowther Library; the State Library of Victoria, including the La Trobe Library; the Tasmanian Museum and Art Gallery, Hobart; the University of Tasmania Archives; Miss P. Finn; Mrs F. Holdsworth and last, but not least, the Archives Office of Tasmania, especially for the staff's time and interest. Thank you also to editors Jane Arms and Louise Sweetland and designer Derrick I. Stone.

Maggie Weidenhofer
Melbourne, 1981

Part of a stone wall at Port Arthur, showing the convicts' pick marks.

This part of the rear wall of the penitentiary shows how the bricks have deterior-
ated since the walls were completed in 1845. The bricks were made at Port
Arthur and the stone was quarried there also.

Introduction

Fifty years after Tasmania was founded in 1803, the colony was in a festive mood. By now the name Van Diemen's Land was unpopular because it was associated with the bondage and guilt of a penal colony, and the name would be changed officially in 1855.[1] On 10 August 1853, the colony's jubilee, the people were celebrating the end of transportation, and according to the *Colonial Times*, 'the "wickedness of the wicked", had ended'.

As if in response to the holiday atmosphere, thick fog lifted from over Hobart Town and climbed the slopes of Mount Wellington, the clouds took a holiday and the Derwent was placid. The bells of Trinity Church pealed, nearly all the shops were closed, and ships and private houses were decorated with flags. While musicians played, thousands of children were entertained, 500 at a time, at tables laden with food and drink, and a 'monster' cake weighing nearly 160 kilograms was cut. Bonfires and fireworks blazed to announce that 'convictism was dead'.

All over the colony the residents celebrated. Into Launceston from early morning came country people—on foot, on horse-back in vehicles of all kinds. Everyone gathered in the city and sang to the tune of 'God Save the Queen':

> Sing! for the hour is come!
> Sing! for our happy home,
>   Our land is free!
> Broken Tasmania's chain;
> Wash'd out the hated stain;
> Ended the strife and pain!
> Blest Jubilee!

Then a huge procession formed of city elders, politicians, horsemen, carriages, a band, native-born colonists and inhabitants and 'others'.

But although the hated stain of transportation had disappeared with the arrival in May 1853 of the last convict ship, the *St Vincent*, convictism lingered. The stain of the convicts was not dead. Nor would it be while the 16 745 males and females in the colony that year continued to serve their sentences, and the penal settlement of Port Arthur existed. Nor would it be while free children screamed 'Tench, Tench!' (penitentiary) at the offspring of transportees.

In 1857, four years after transportation ended, the census revealed that 50 per cent of adults and 60 per cent of adult males were convicts or ex-convicts. By the mid 1860s, the colony's prisons, hospitals and charitable institutions were crowded with more prisoners, invalids and paupers than South Australia and Queensland had together. Even as late as 1889, most of the 800 paupers in the colony's institutions had originally been transportees. By 1891, the *Tasmanian Official Record* noted with some satisfaction 'how remarkably fast the old foreign element in our Gaols and Pauper Establishments is dying out'.[2]

The penal settlement of Port Arthur, established in 1830 on Tasman Peninsula, was soon the only settlement in the colony—and it became to Tasmania what the colony was to Britain: a prison without walls. Misery of 'the deepest dye' existed at Port Arthur. Nevertheless, though some newspaper editors of the 1830s condemned it as worse than death in an attempt to discredit Lieut.-Governor George Arthur, who wanted to control the press, for most of its history the settlement was not as severe a penal settlement as Macquarie Harbour, which Arthur himself described as 'a last alternation, next to capital punishment'.

The Tasman Peninsula settlement was intended to put the fear of God into convicts in the colony, accommodate the worst and deter others from crime. Its reputation was such that in 1841, Lieut.-Governor Sir John Franklin wrote to his superiors that 'there is something so lowering...attached to the name of a Port Arthur man'.[3] Once one had been a 'Port Arthur man', it seems there was no escape from the tag. In the late 1870s, a visitor noted that 'Port Arthur waifs' who had settled on the north-west coast of the colony 'must remain under suspicion until the end of their days...Young Tasmania cannot forgive those of a former generation who bear the convict brand'.[4]

Exactly how many prisoners were sentenced to Port Arthur will not be known until the record of each male convict in the colony between 1830 and 1877 is examined—about 61 000 records, including those of a few thousand men from New South Wales, Norfolk Island and elsewhere, and some colonial-born men. However, an estimated figure of 12 700 men is said to be not unreasonable. These would not all have been sentenced to transportation; after 1855, following the introduction of the Penal Servitude Act, the term 'penal servitude', not 'transportation', was used.

By the early 1860s, most of the prisoners at Port Arthur were the dregs of a criminal population whose reformation was said by Governor Thomas Gore Brown to be hopeless, but perfect order was maintained at the settlement without violence.[5] Of 492 convicts there, 108 had been convicted more than three times in the colony's courts, 165 two to four times,

199 one to three times and 20 once only. The British government, in the late 1860s, considered that Port Arthur was one of its better prisons, the others being in Barbados, British Guiana, Canada, Malta, Queensland and South Australia. At the time it was said that the settlement 'is beginning to be regarded as a model in other Australian Colonies, and it may become of great service in this respect'.[6]

Encouraged by Marcus Clarke's novel, *For the Term of His Natural Life*, the 'worse than death' description of conditions at the settlement have lingered. But punishment eased in the late 1840s, and even more so in the 1850s, in response to new approaches to penal discipline in Britain, which were thought to be more humane than flogging. According to official policy, the prisoners' treatment was still harsh, but worse punishments were employed elsewhere—for example, at Sing Sing in the United States.

Long after transportation ceased, Port Arthur was continuing to receive reconvicted transportees and also colonial-born criminals. By the late 1850s, when the new penitentiary was opened, bed-space remained in the huts that formed the decrepit old penitentiary and into these huts tottered the destitute, the infirm and the mentally ill from other institutions. Even so, the settlement, which could accommodate well over a thousand men, had become a white elephant by 1869, too costly to maintain for dwindling numbers of men. In that year it was suggested that Port Arthur could be 'the one great Benevolent and Invalid Institute' for Tasmania, but the settlement remained much as it was.[7]

Finally, in 1877, most of the prisoners were transferred to the Hobart gaol, while the other men were sent to the appropriate institutions, where many of them lived out their last days. Even in the early twentieth century, some ex-convicts were still alive, their backs striped with the scars of floggings. One old man had been determined to remain at the settlement when it closed, and several returned and became guides to the growing number of tourists who came to wonder at the remnants of that place of misery in its beautiful setting. As the years passed, some of the tales the men told were embroidered with fancy stitches and they were believed to have manufactured souvenir leg-irons of a weight greater than any used at Port Arthur.

The name Port Arthur, which was changed officially to Carnarvon in 1877, rapidly returned to favour because it was the old penal settlement ruins that attracted visitors to the town.[8] There were some Tasmanians who wanted to deny Port Arthur's existence, but others recognized its tourist potential, which grew year by year. Before the end of the century, fires sweeping through the buildings set back tentative attempts to provide for visitors, but soon Port Arthur began to thrive again. A museum, a hotel, tea-rooms, and guest-houses provided for tourists, who came by horse-drawn carriages or steamers.

By the late 1920s, Marcus Clarke's novel had been filmed on location at Port Arthur, with many local people—some who still live nearby—acting as 'extras'. The film proved to be a further boost to tourism, and the Scenery Preservation Board began to restore some of the ruins. Over the decades, interest in Port Arthur has not faltered. The number of Australian and overseas visitors has grown to a quarter of a million annually, drawn irresistibly to the Port Arthur Historic Site, which is in the care of the National Parks and Wildlife Service.

1   An Important Public Benefit

Spectacular columnar structures, Capes Raoul and Pillar rise straight from the sea and form ranges of lofty cliffs that glower at the surging Tasman Sea. Their basaltic prisms resemble crumbling ruins or stacks of chimneys; some lean like the Tower of Pisa. Between these capes, in November 1827, the *Opossum* sailed to seek a safe anchorage during stormy weather en route to Hobart Town from Maria Island on the east coast, and found it in Stewart's Harbour. The ship's captain, John Welsh, investigated the harbour and, impressed with the abundant timber lining its shores, he returned to Hobart, where he reported that the area was 'a desirable situation for a secondary kind of penal settlement'.[1] The words implied that the Lieut.-Governor, Colonel George Arthur, needed a suitable site for a third penal settlement for convicts who had committed crimes after their arrival in the colony.

Welsh's visit to the harbour led to Port Arthur's founding, because a month later, when a replacement for a convict sawing station at Birch's Bay was being discussed, Stewart's Harbour on Tasman Peninsula was immediately considered. To the young and growing colony a large and continuing supply of timber for public works was vital, so Welsh was sent back with a survey team to report on the quality and quantity of timber, as well as the availability of water. A well-behaved convict sawyer accompanied the team to give his opinion about the timber.

The team recommended a bay to the south of Stewart's

The entrance to Port Arthur, between Capes Raoul, at left, and Pillar, with Tasman Island to the right of Cape Pillar.

Lieut.-Governor George Arthur, after whom Port Arthur was named.

Harbour, asking permission to name it Port Arthur, 'which we do from profound respect'. They reported: 'Should this be a Penal settlement (for which we think it is well adapted), we beg to recommend the bay ... being in the centre of the forest, having a good run of water and shelter from all winds.' Quantities of gum, stringybark, myrtle, lightwood and sassafras grew near the shore and appeared to be of good quality. Felling and sawing the timber could keep any number of convicts occupied for several years, and it could easily be loaded on to ships until after the trees nearest the harbour's edge had been felled.

In April 1828, having decided to establish a sawing station at Stewart's Harbour, Arthur asked for immediate arrangements for the gradual abandonment of Birch's Bay station and for boats to take well-conducted convicts to Stewart's Harbour, where they would erect huts for the new settlement. In December, however, Port Arthur had not been founded and the harbour was being surveyed for the second time, by Deputy Surveyor-General Thomas Scott. Like Welsh, he was impressed with the timber and thought that for a few years convicts rather than bullocks could haul it to the water's edge. Scott also reported on the likelihood of prisoners being able to escape from Wedge Bay, where whaling and fishing boats anchored, as well as the possible danger to security of a farm—the only one on the peninsula—owned by the former Attorney-General, Joseph Tice Gellibrand.[2]

Meanwhile, the situation between the Aborigines and the colonists had continued to deteriorate and between 1828 and 1830 Arthur's preoccupation with attempting to find a solution delayed the founding of Port Arthur. The military was deployed to strategic points to protect settlers and, eventually, on 9 September 1830, Arthur called on the entire population of Tasmania to form a line in order to capture the Aborigines or to drive them across Eaglehawk Neck on to Tasman Peninsula.

The operation would begin on 7 October.[3] Within a few days of this announcement, Arthur ordered the founding of Port Arthur, and by January the following year he was considering the possibility of leaving the rest of Tasman Peninsula open to 'the free and unmolested occupancy of the Aborigines'.[4]

The news of Port Arthur's founding was reported by the *Tasmanian & Austral-Asiatic Review*, which praised the government for spreading the population to an important sea-point, 'by which a communication will be speedily opened with Hobart-town through a very valuable, but hitherto little known country'. The settlement would be 'an important public benefit', the *Review* continued enthusiastically, and 'an intermediate sort of penal place of employment between the extreme misery of Macquarie Harbour, and the somewhat less so of the Hobart prisoners barracks'.[5] The name Macquarie Harbour needed no qualification. Founded in 1822 on the isolated, rugged west coast, battered by the Roaring Forties, it was 'associated exclusively with ... inexpressible depravity, degradation, and woe'.[6] It was one of two penal settlements at the time, the other being Darlington at Maria Island, which was established in 1825 for prisoners convicted of less serious crimes.

In the past, the commandants of Macquarie Harbour had wanted to lessen the punishment of some of their 'incorrigibles', as well as over-crowding at the settlement, by returning them to what were known as the settled districts. Arthur had not been enthusiastic about the suggestion. In March 1831, when he informed the Secretary of State, Sir George Murray, of the formation and location of Port Arthur, he explained how cautious he had been about removing prisoners from the west coast settlement, 'lest the salutary dread in which the punishment [there] is held should in any degree be lessened'. Instead, at moderate expense, he had founded Port Arthur as a combined penal settlement for men reconvicted of minor crimes and as a sawing station, to which Macquarie Harbour prisoners could be sent for further probation. At the same time he described how the new settlement was situated at a convenient distance from Hobart and how secure Port Arthur was.[7]

Once the decision had been made to open Port Arthur, the authorities moved quickly. At Birch's Bay, the prisoners selected for the new settlement, including an overseer, two timber-fellers, four sawyers, five shingle-splitters and a shoemaker, were to prepare to leave and to take their clothing, bedding and tools, and at Hobart, six weeks' provisions for an officer, fifteen soldiers and fifty prisoners were loaded on to the *Derwent*.[8] A commandant, Dr John Russell, was appointed, and the importance of his duties impressed upon him. The assistant surgeon of the 63rd Regiment, Russell had had various civil and military duties which included being the surgeon at the Launceston hospital, and he would remain at Port Arthur until July the following year, during which time he carried out the duties of surgeon and chaplain. His earliest duties would be to prepare a plan of the settlement, which would allow for extension in the future, and a list of regulations.

A late nineteenth-century panorama of Port Arthur, showing the settlement in the centre foreground. The entrance to Long Bay is at the far left and next to it is the present-day Stewart Harbour. The Isle of the Dead is opposite Point Puer.

On 20 September 1830, the *Derwent* anchored in an inlet of the 'fine capacious harbour in which a large fleet might ride in safety sheltered from every wind'. As the best position for the settlement, Russell chose the inlet opposite Opossum Island (named after Captain Welsh's ship and later to be renamed Isle de Mort or Isle of the Dead). While the *Derwent* lay at anchor, the crew and prisoners cleared thick scrub and tall trees on the land where huts were to be erected. They hauled the felled timber to the newly established sawpits, where it was sawed for building purposes.[9]

Almost immediately the settlement ran into difficulties. Regularly, Russell attempted to obtain stores and often had to repeat his orders. No wonder then that he wrote tartly to his superiors: 'The many inconveniences ... will naturally appear to any person who gives the subject the least consideration'. The stores he requested in November 1830 were delayed after the ordnance officer complained at length to the Colonial Secretary, John Burnett, that Russell's order 'far exceeds any Requisitions I have ever been called on to comply with. ... The Requisitions occupied seven pages. Within a few weeks I have had to discharge and dispose of ... the Cargoes of *Five* Convict Ships and the present operation against the Natives has considerably augmented my duties'.[10]

While the ordnance office went its way, the prisoners' most basic needs were seemingly forgotten in Hobart. 'Men are nearly naked, having come down here destitute of the most essential articles for the formation of a Settlement,' Russell wrote to his superiors after a ship arrived at Port Arthur without clothing and tools.[11] But one of his greatest problems in those early months was the scale of the men's rations. The staples in the diet were bread and gruel. Breakfast and supper consisted of bread, gruel and tea, and dinner was bread, salt meat and soup. Vinegar was also distributed because so many prisoners had scurvy, particularly boys sent direct to the settlement after the long voyage from England.

The scale of rations caused a great deal of discontent and grumbling among prisoners who claimed that although they had been led to believe that they were going to Port Arthur not as a punishment but as an indulgence, they were receiving less food than they had at Birch's Bay, Macquarie Harbour and in road parties. Different classes of convicts in the colony were given different scales of rations, and Russell was in the embarrassing position of not knowing how much extra food the men should have, if any, apart from what they persuaded him they were entitled to. They begged him to approach the government on their behalf, which he did, but nothing could be done while Arthur was away coping with 'the important operations against the Hostile Aborigines'.[12] Meanwhile, had the prisoners mutinied, Russell and his small band of soldiers would have stood little chance against them and had no way of immediately calling for reinforcements from Hobart. It is to Russell's credit that he was able to contain what he later described to the Select Committee on Transportation in 1837 as 'a mutinous feeling ... but I soon quelled it; nothing serious'.

At such an isolated, poorly equipped settlement as Port Arthur was during Russell's command—and during the terms of his successors, Captain John Mahon and Lieut. John Gibbons—the abilities to improvise and compromise were vital. For example, as Russell was limited in his resources, he allowed the prisoners to fish and to have small garden plots for vegetables. In the 1840s, an interesting description of gardening and fishing at Port Arthur in the early years was given by a convict superintendent:

Many of [the prisoners] would work late and early, and would often finish their work by middle day Friday; they would then work in their gardens, or go fishing; and as fish abound in the bays, they would catch enough for the whole settlement; and as we had ... scarcely anything but salt meat and very little vegetables, we found the fish very acceptable. The men were in much better health, better behaved, better tempered, and many of them were very industrious men. There was scarcely any flogging, very little punishment of any sort and the feeling between the officers and the prisoners was of a kindly nature.[13]

Russell also allowed the officers to fish, partly because they were jealous when the prisoners fished and, as he told the Select Committee, 'I rather encouraged it for the sake of safety' in case the convicts should attempt to escape.

Despite Russell's attempts to improve nutrition, scurvy continued to be a major problem, which Captain Mahon inherited in July 1831 when he became commandant. The number of prisoners had increased to about 150 and at least a quarter of them had scurvy, 'some of them seriously ill but who continue to exert themselves'. Twice Mahon asked for live, fat sheep to be sent as often as possible to supplement the salt meat rations, and eventually he got them, and he also asked for fresh supplies for at least six days a month. Commendable though Mahon's concern was for health and diet, it tended to relate to the settlement's productivity: 'The Scurvy . . . has been serious and still is so; it continues a draw back on the Industry of the Settlement'.[14]

The primitive hospital was 'in the most wretched state of poverty'. At times Mahon had to send men to Hobart for treatment. Once, when an urgent case arose, 'a piece of whale bone had to be cut up and introduced at all hazards—instead of the usual "Bougie" [surgical instrument] to save the man's life who was troubled with strictures'.[15] Genuine cases of illness were frequent, but to compound the problem, two men feigned sickness in order to be sent to Hobart, where the surgeon reported indignantly that the acting surgeon at Port Arthur was

Part of Port Arthur's first orders and regulations, drawn up by the Commandant, Dr John Russell, in 1831. They were not as extensive as the regulations would become in the future.

Orders & Regulations

for the Government & Management of the Settlement at

Port Arthur

Rules to be Observed by the Convicts

No 1 — Quiet and Orderly Conduct will be considered at all times absolutely necessary, with strict Obedience to all Persons placed in Authority over them.

2 — The Men will live and Mess in those Huts within the Enclosure of the Prisoners Barracks, which are allotted to them, & in no others. The Huts are Calculated to Contain Twelve Men each, and the Boys Barracks Twenty four.

3 — The Convicts at Port Arthur are divided into three Classes.

Viz:

1 — Those that are well conducted have the Privilege of going any where within Bounds during daylight after the hours of Work, & during the afternoon of Saturday and during Sunday.

2 — Those, for Misconduct, sentenced to Work in Irons who will be employed during the Afternoon of Saturday at any Work which may be required, & when not at Work are to be confined to Barracks.

3 — Those in the Gaol gang, for more Serious Offences. They will be confined in the Cell when not at Work; and will be employed as those of the 2nd Class on Saturday afternoon.

4 — The Prisoners will retire to Bed at Nine O'clock in Summer and at Eight in Winter, but after the Evening Muster no Man is to be out of his Hut.

5 — The Men will be held responsible for the Cleanliness and regularity of the Huts which they inhabit, and each Man of his own Berth

'altogether incompetent for his duties'. As the prisoners' cure, Arthur recommended a little discipline in the chain-gang at Hobart.[16]

Not the least of each of the commandant's difficulties was the lack of prisoners able to carry out the labour of felling, sawing and similar tasks. Although all of the first batch of prisoners were apparently qualified, soon some of them left after serving their terms at the settlement. Others would arrive who were sometimes unsuited for tasks that were essential for shelter for the settlement and for fulfilling orders from town for timber to be used for important public works. On one occasion, near the end of 1830, of twenty-five prisoners who arrived, twenty-two were boys sent specifically to work with the sawyers as an experiment. Concerned, Russell complained that their unannounced arrival was rather premature because he had not had time to prepare for them and asked if more boys would be sent. Although Arthur replied that he would wait to see the result of the experiment, he gave Russell permission to have the boys taught appropriate trades.[17]

Orders for timber became so large and at times the prisoners suited to the labour were so few that for several years a man's usefulness, not his crime, could be the reason for his despatch to Port Arthur. Some men, after being transported, had acquired the trades needed—for instance, at Macquarie Harbour or Birch's Bay—and all had had diverse occupations in Britain such as coachman and groom, hairdresser, labourer, letterpress printer, sailmaker, sweep and rat-catcher, watch-key maker and well-sinker. In desperation, the commandants would request men with particular skills. Russell asked for two carpenters for three months because at the time he had only one—a former Macquarie Harbour wood-cutter who described himself as a 'rough carpenter' but was totally ignorant of the trade and useless. A few months later, in 1831, when the Engineer's Department sent a large, unspecific order for wood, Russell

became annoyed. What sort of wood? he asked. Furthermore, to saw the timber would take a year and a half with the six pairs of sawyers at the settlement. 'Should there be any great urgency, it would be well to send a few more Sawyers.' None could be spared, although the wood was required for a school for female orphans, which was eventually completed in 1833.[18]

While Mahon also asked for sawyers and carpenters, his other requests for men with particular skills—for example, brickmakers and charcoal-burners—reflected the diversification of activities at the settlement. Yet it continued principally as a sawing station, and throughout 1831 hundreds of thousands of shingles for roofs and 63 000 metres of sawn timber were exported to Hobart, as well as wooden products such as brooms, wheelbarrows, buckets, lamp posts and cart-spokes.[19] In the following year, charcoal and sun-dried bricks were supplied, and also men's and boy's boots and women's and girls' shoes made by convict shoemakers who had been sent to Port Arthur to work for the government, because it had been impossible to prevent them from illegally making and selling for their own profit.[20]

The first prisoners included young boys and men newly arrived from Britain, as well as old hands who had been at Macquarie Harbour or elsewhere in the colony for some years. According to Russell's evidence to the Select Committee in 1837, the new arrivals were a tolerably manageable set, but the more hardened offenders soon exercised 'a complete tyranny over them', causing them to become 'as hardened, as reckless, and as hypocritical as they were themselves'. The new prisoners learnt from the old hands to approach Russell with 'a countenance characteristic of innocence, while they were perhaps plotting mischief'. Minor crimes were punished at the settlement, and serious ones were tried at the Supreme Court in Hobart, and some men who knew nothing about a crime would offer evidence in the hope of getting away from Port

When timber near the harbour was cleared, the convicts penetrated further inland on Tasman Peninsula into country similar to this. Up to seventy men would carry a huge log and these gangs became known as Centipedes. Horses and bullocks were not used at Port Arthur or nearby until the 1860s.

Eaglehawk Neck, the isthmus between Tasman and Forestier peninsulas, with Eaglehawk Bay at left and Pirates Bay, right. The bush is less dense than it was in the early 1830s, when some convicts attempted to evade the guards and make their way back to the colony.

Arthur. 'I recollect playing a trick on them', Russell continued, 'by spreading a report . . . that I was about to commit a man for trial for some offence to the Supreme Court, and I obtained all the necessary evidence by that means, and . . . I punished the case myself summarily afterwards.' On the other hand, sometimes it was difficult for him to obtain evidence because there was a strong spirit of honour among thieves which prevented them from informing on each other. (Attempting to leave the settlement by this means or by committing crimes was not peculiar to Port Arthur men and occurred at Macquarie Harbour and Norfolk Island.)

When appointed as commandant, Russell had been told:

In order to possess the necessary control over prisoners, which the certain and prompt punishment of their misconduct can alone insure His Excellency will be happy to place you in the Commission of the Peace, but he is very desirous, that in the discharge of the important Magisterial functions which will thus devolve upon you that you should avoid, as much as it is possible, the instigation of two descriptions of punishment, for the same offence . . . and His Excellency hopes by the execution of some strong and Secure Solitary cells and their frequent use for the punishment of . . . Offences that you will Seldom find it necessary to resort to Corporal punishment.[21]

But Russell had difficulty in carrying out the instructions because there were no solitary cells for some time. His solution was to remove the leg-irons of every prisoner who arrived and make the wearing of them a punishment. At the same time, the man in irons would be confined to the settlement itself and, between the hours of labour, to a small gaol—a punishment the prisoners dreaded.[22] The use of the lash was resorted to, but not as frequently nor as severely as at Macquarie Harbour—the settlement Arthur described as 'a last alternation, next to capital punishment'—where one hundred lashes or more were common. In 1830 at Port Arthur, however, when the maximum number of prisoners was sixty-eight, the average number of lashes was nineteen, inflicted on five men, and in 1832, when the population had risen to 280, seventy-two men received an average of forty-six lashes each.[23]

Absconding was a particularly serious crime and by 1832 thirty-five prisoners had escaped. The prescribed bounds of the settlement, as laid down by Russell in the first regulations, were: 'Stewart's Bay to the Northward, The Rocky Point near the Brick kilns in Opossum Bay to the Southward, and one Mile from the Settlement in any other Direction.' But so many prisoners were working in gangs in the bush outside this area that it was sometimes not difficult for them to slip away undetected.[24]

In an attempt to deter escapees, Mahon sent four sawyers and a boat builder to Hobart for trial instead of punishing them himself, but in no time four more men were being pursued by the military on the peninsula.[25] The opportunity to leave Port Arthur, either permanently or for a trial, was welcomed by the prisoners, so sending them to town was unlikely to be a deterrent. Consequently, the settlement's punishments for this offence had to be, and were, severe. Gibbons, who succeeded Mahon in August 1832, described the punishments to his superiors:

the severest description of labour with Corporal Punishment is invariably visited upon those Convicts who abscond ... heavy double Irons, carrying Sawed Timber from the Saw pits to the Settlement, sometimes a distance of half and three quarters of a mile, or working incessantly in a quarry during the day.... I ... submit that I do not think that any severer mode of punishment can be adopted.

Clearly, Arthur agreed that the punishments were adequate. After reading Gibbons's letter, he noted on it: 'Nor is it necessary I should think.'[26]

The best solution to the growing number of escapees was to have an impassable barrier at Eaglehawk Neck, a narrow isthmus about 70 metres at the narrowest part. It was the only land outlet from Tasman Peninsula to the colony. In 1831,

---

A reward notice in the Hobart Town Gazette, *February 1833. Thomas Semes was recaptured and transported to Norfolk Island; Perkins was returned to Port Arthur, where he died in 1839.*

Russell evidently had in mind placing a guard there when he sent a plan and description of the isthmus to his superiors, and Mahon had recommended the same. The result was that by the end of 1831, soldiers of the 63rd Regiment were guarding both East Bay Neck (between Forestier Peninsula and the mainland) and Eaglehawk Neck, and within a few months all the soldiers were concentrated at the latter, which was more appropriate for intercepting escapees.[27]

Placing sentries at Eaglehawk Neck was only the first step towards its complete security, because in 1832 a soldier in command there, Ensign John Peyton Jones, put forward an ingenious suggestion that was to make the isthmus an effective barrier for more than forty years. He wrote:

It occurred to me that the only way to prevent the escape of Prisoners from Port Arthur in consequence of the noise occasioned by the continual roar of the Sea breaking on the beach and the peculiar formation of the Land which rendered Sentries comparatively useless, was to establish a line of Lamps and Dogs—I therefore at once covered a way with cockle shells so as to shew a brilliant light on the ground at night, and proposed that a certain number of dogs (9) to be so placed that they could not fight although eat out of the same trough, and render it impossible for anyone to pass through.

By September 1832, Arthur had despatched a schooner with dogs and equipment, and according to Peyton Jones, 'so effective was the arrangement that during 16 months I was there, no man ever crossed the neck.'[28]

Within a few years, in the 1830s, eleven dogs were spaced across the isthmus, one was on a platform in Norfolk Bay close to the Port Arthur road, and others were on the surf beach of Pirates Bay. Near the dogs on the isthmus were nine lamps on posts raised about a metre above the ground, enabling the sentries to observe the dogs. Those convicts who managed to cross the Neck at this time kept to the surf, where they were less likely to be seen.[29]

A rare early view of Eaglehawk Neck, the guards and guard dogs, by John Peyton Jones. In 1832, nine dogs were placed across the Neck and on a platform in Eaglehawk Bay, but later the number of dogs was extended to about eighteen. They became an effective barrier to escape for more than forty years.

2   A Place for Everybody . . .

During 1832 plans were underway to close Maria Island and Macquarie Harbour penal settlements and to establish Port Arthur as the only settlement in Tasmania, rather than continue the expense of maintaining two 'imperfect' settlements. The reasons for closing Maria Island, which had been established for convicts who had committed less serious offences, were simpler than those for Macquarie Harbour, but the east coast settlement was somewhat isolated, too far from government supervision, and escapes had been frequent. It was closed in September. The west coast settlement, however, was so inaccessible that voyages from Hobart could last as long as two months, and the bar at the entrance to the harbour was filling up, making navigation increasingly hazardous; it was also too far from government supervision; plans to open nearby country to settlers would make escape easier; and the type of employment for the convicts was limited, preventing different degrees of severity.[1]

Like Maria Island, Port Arthur had been receiving prisoners reconvicted of minor offences, as well as Macquarie Harbour men on probation, but in the future it was planned to send more serious offenders there. But the plans to close Macquarie Harbour first required a thorough assessment of Port Arthur, because a Select Committee had reported to Arthur in November that Port Arthur must be made as secure as the west coast settlement and have at least one grade of punishment equally severe.[2] So in December Arthur embarked on the *Isabella* to make his first inspection of the Tasman Peninsula settlement, and within a few days he returned to Hobart to list the initial improvements he felt were necessary.

Although Arthur was generally satisfied with the state of the settlement, changes were essential. He decided, for example, that every convict must wear yellow clothing, because it was distinctive and other clothing facilitated escape. Private gardens were 'most objectionable' and were to be replaced by one large settlement vegetable garden for labour, not recreation. A large commissariat store was to be built, and also a timber yard at the water's edge so that contact between the prisoners and boat crews and the opportunity for the delivery or the despatch of letters would be avoided. Correspondence was prohibited, except for memorials and petitions ('no matter how improper the style and manner') to the government. 'Idlers'—watchmen, wardsmen, cooks, servants and clerks—were to be chosen only from well-behaved prisoners. The large number of shoemakers were not to be employed by private individuals, and military and civil officers who required shoes and boots had to pay a fair price to the government. Commandant Gibbons was asked to prepare an outline of new regulations.[3]

Further improvements would soon be suggested by officers in Hobart whom Arthur had approached. One important suggestion from the Port Officer, William Moriarty, con-

---

Part of a Hobart chain-gang in James Backhouses's book, A Narrative of a Visit to the Australian Colonies, *in which he describes his visits to Port Arthur in the early 1830s.*

A map of Tasmania.

Launceston

Macquarie
Harbour

HOBART   Maria
Island

Tasman
Peninsula

Port Arthur

cerned the classification of convicts: 'to make Port Arthur fully capable of carrying on the discipline necessary for either the punishment or reformation of the prisoner . . . it will be necessary to establish a proper classification . . . and there should be one gang work[ing] constantly in chains'. Having a convict superintendent was unsatisfactory, and a free and respectable man should be appointed, a man of 'firm, temperate and energetic habits', who could 'check insubordination without giving way to violence, and sufficiently active to stimulate by his own example, feelings which in even so degraded a caste, are not . . . utterly extinct'.[4]

In a flurry of activity, Arthur sent instructions to Macquarie Harbour for its abandonment and devised new regulations for Port Arthur, writing despatches to London to justify his plans. But by April 1833 the commandant of the west coast settlement, Pery Baylee, had not replied to three letters about its closure from his superiors, who were 'displeased' because they had learnt about the building of a new brig there contrary to orders. The *Frederick* was all absorbing and was delaying the settlement's closure. Finally, in November 1833, the settlement was abandoned, except for a group remaining to finish the brig. Then a drama occurred that increased the authorities' displeasure: in January the *Frederick* was seized by the twelve convict shipwrights and sailors on board, and eventually the news filtered back to the colony that the mutineers had reached Valdivia in Chile in March 1834.[5]

Meanwhile, in February 1833, unaware that Macquarie Harbour's closure would be so protracted, Arthur wrote frequent, voluminous despatches to London about its abandonment and the advantages of Tasman Peninsula as a natural penitentiary and sent a plan that showed how well suited it was for the purposes of penal discipline. At the same time he enclosed the new 'Standing Instructions for the Regulation of the Penal Settlement on Tasman's Peninsula' and an explanation of each class of his system of convict discipline for the whole colony, of which Port Arthur was about to become a vital part. 'My Lord', Arthur wrote, 'the facilities afforded by this colony for carrying classification into effect are such as never could be attained within the walls of a penitentiary' in England.[6]

So pleased was Arthur with the 1833 regulations for Port Arthur that he went so far as to suggest that if they were 'extensively circulated in England, His Majesty's Government may thereby revive those terrors of transportation which it is supposed have been lost since these colonies have so rapidly advanced in wealth and importance; and it is my conviction that Van Diemen's Land may be made a terror to evil doers for the next quarter of a century at least'. The regulations revealed that Port Arthur would feature 'the most unceasing labour . . . and the most harrassing vigilance' together with 'a minute system of classification', intended to develop the prisoners' characters, habits and dispositions, and not only reform the criminals themselves but deter others from crime.[7]

The system of convict discipline comprised seven classes: tickets-of-leave (class 1); assignment in the service of the settlers (class 2); employment in the public departments or public works (class 3); road gangs (class 4); chain-gangs (class 5); penal settlements (class 6); and chain-gangs within the penal settlements (class 7). The convicts' classification depended on conduct. For example, if a convict in assignment became 'indolent, quarrelsome and vicious, or in any way sets a bad example to his fellow-servants', he was moved to another class. The result was, wrote Arthur, that according to his offence or offences, he was sent to a road party, a chain-gang, or perhaps a penal settlement. In this way there was a continual circulation of convicts throughout the colony, 'a distribution of each in his appropriate place', and the process of classification depended not on the authority of the government, but on the prisoners themselves.[8]

According to a description of the system, drawn up by the Principal Superintendent of Convicts, Josiah Spode, a ticket-of-leave was the great reward aimed for and a convict who 'bids fair to make an atonement for his former misdeeds' could obtain one after good conduct over a certain number of years. The ticket allowed comparative freedom, enabling the convict to work for himself and move from one district to another providing he had permission and reported at regular musters. Allotting tickets caused Arthur hours of work because he considered the application of every convict and made the final decision.[9]

In contrast to ticket-of-leavers, in assignment (class 2) a convict worked for a master, who gave him rations and clothing according to a government scale. He had less freedom than a ticket-of-leave man but a period of good conduct brought with it 'the enjoyment' of a ticket. If he misbehaved and was reprimanded, flogged or spent time in the stocks or on the treadwheel, all to no avail, he would be removed to another class in the system. For example in the public works (class 3), a well-behaved man would be loaned to settlers for limited periods to help erect buildings and various works in the colony, but for repeated misconduct he would be moved to another class, perhaps a road gang (class 4). Throughout the colony, roads were being built and kept in repair by convicts in this class, whose offences were not serious enough to subject them to a chain-gang. Yet they worked constantly for long hours with pick, spade, and barrow and lived in rough huts as close as possible to their work, receiving limited government rations.

By the time a man was transferred to the chain-gang (class 5), he had experienced almost every minor punishment in vain. Many men in this class had received colonial sentences of transportation to a penal settlement, but the sentence had been commuted and saved the expense of maintaining them at a settlement. Day and night this class wore double leg-irons, which varied in weight according to the offence or the man's 'hardihood'. They broke stones for repairing roads and wheeled them in barrows, while a gang of the most depraved did the heaviest and severest labour. The only passport from this wretched state was the 'utmost good conduct; every fresh offence prolongs the servitude and renders less chance of relief'.

At the penal settlements (class 6), which soon would be one settlement—Port Arthur—were men who had been reconvicted after their arrival in the colony, those whose offences before their arrival had been 'of an atrocious nature', those whose offences during the voyage required a marked example, and those educated convicts whose behaviour had compelled the government to give them 'a most rigid course of correction'. Although all punishment at a settlement was severe, a special class (class 7) comprised the chain-gangs—those men whose crime warranted a sentence to work in leg-irons or whose misconduct at the settlement required their removal from another gang. The chain-gang work was of 'the most incessant and galling description the settlement can produce, and any disobedience of orders, turbulence or other misconduct, is instantaneously punished by the lash'. At the other end of the scale, to allow hope to men at a penal settlement, there were relief gangs for those who had conducted themselves satisfactorily. From these gangs were chosen those most fitting and deserving for subordinate offices such as watchmen, cooks, and servants.

The new Port Arthur regulations of 1833 actually dealt in more detail with the duties of the commandant, police magistrate, surgeon, chaplain, superintendent of convicts, commissariat officer and officers generally than it did with the prisoners themselves. But the labour of the convicts was clearly spelt out—hewing and cutting timber and hauling it to the harbour, erecting buildings, ploughing and cultivating land, and making

In the mid 1840s, in Tasmania, road gangs lived in prefabricated timber huts, which were completely self-contained. When the gang moved to another site, the men carried the huts, fittings, bedding and so on, but transport waggons were used for long distances.

roads—and with few exceptions all convicts at the settlement carried out these duties. (Decades would pass before beasts of burden such as bullock teams would be introduced at Port Arthur. It was calculated that five men carrying timber were the equal of a bullock team and driver.) Most prisoners wore yellow government-issue clothing, but that of the chain-gang men was distinguished by the word felon stamped on it. Chain-

Convicts during a rest period.

gang men slept in separate cells, wearing their leg-irons, went to work in Indian file and were permitted no conversation.

Lighter work was performed by invalids and well-behaved educated men, as well as prisoners removed to a relief gang. In the latter, grey clothing was worn, the work was constant but less severe and was often in agriculture and horticulture. Educated convicts, however, who also wore grey clothing, were employed in gardening, fencing and farming at the settlement and under strict surveillance, as were all prisoners. Their punishment was similar to that of the other men—hard labour, removal to the chain-gang, flagellation or whatever best suited the circumstances.

In the words of the Colonial Secretary, John Burnett, educated convicts (or gentlemen convicts, as they were often called)—solicitors, doctors, clergymen, architects—were to be separated from the rest of the community and placed at Port Arthur, where they would not have 'victims upon whom their superior cunning will enable them to prey, and that intelligence which they have so miserably abused and misdirected, will not avail them'. Although this class had not caused as many problems to Arthur as they had in Sydney, he had decided to despatch all those guilty of misconduct to the settlement. However, even if those in Tasmania had had influence, it was unlikely that they could 'ever turn it to any great account to the injury of the Government or the public', he wrote, 'even if they were inclined to do so'.

They were a nuisance, he thought, because they were 'ill-conducted, and their reformation is perhaps more hopeless than that of any other class, insomuch as they are usually confirmed drunkards'. Some had been employed in public offices, 'a practice which I exceedingly deprecate, as they do little work, and are disposed to embezzle the public property in order to purchase drink'. Arthur disagreed with the view that educated men should not be put to hard labour nor reduced in status to that of the illiterate or common criminal, because they were physically weaker and would feel the privations more, though it was not fair that individuals should be punished differently for similar offences.

At Port Arthur educated men would not hear of matters not for their ears, or walk about town dressed as gentlemen, or write letters to friends in England 'holding up the brighter side of the picture' of their life in Tasmania.[10] Merely one letter from one of these men could 'deprive transportation of much of its terrors', and apparently Stanley de Courcey Ireland (alias Samuel Wilson), a barrister transported for life for high treason, was guilty of this offence. In 1832, while at Port Arthur, he wrote indignantly to the authorities:

By some unaccountable mistake I have been sent to Port Arthur, and classed among the very sweepings of all the penal Settlements, Gaols, and Penitentiaries of Van Diemen's Land: in my own defence (always an unpleasant duty) I must say I did not deserve such treatment....

His petition to leave the settlement did not impress Arthur: 'let him be informed that some of his letters to his friends in England have fallen into the hands of the Government at Home and will explain to him why he has been detained [there].'[11] Nor was the Colonial Secretary, Burnett, moved when a police magistrate commented on educated men at Port Arthur: 'I was much struck with their appearance ... they ... appear to feel most acutely the Misery and Degradation.' Before passing on the letter to Arthur, Burnett noted sarcastically in the margin, 'This is indeed worse than death!'[12]

Many convicts spent more time in a penal settlement than not and many of them were petty thieves who circulated regularly among the colony's classes of punishment—'each in his appropriate place'. William Yeomans was one of them. He was among 73 500 men and women who were transported to Tasmania and among the total 162 000 convicts who arrived in Australia. More than half of the total had been sentenced to seven years' transportation, as he was; about a quarter were sentenced to life (although the proportion of lifers decreased over the years); and most of the remainder received fourteen-year sentences until 1840, after which ten-year sentences were quite common. Before 1840, most of the first offenders went to New South Wales, but those with worse records or guilty of more serious crimes arrived in Tasmania, where the proportion of recorded first offenders was less than an eighth of that in New South Wales.[13]

Larceny—Yeomans's crime—was by far the most common crime of all transportees and more than nine-tenths of all convicts had been guilty of some form of theft such as breaking and entering, burglary, highway robbery with violence, picking pockets, stealing livestock, or shoplifting. Half or probably two-thirds had been punished in Britain, usually for forms of larceny. After arrival in Tasmania, convict men averaged five punishments each, one in ten was convicted for a serious offence before the superior courts of the colony, and another 10 per cent were apparently never punished at all.[14]

In 1830, William Yeomans arrived in Tasmania as a seven-year man—the worst and most incorrigible class of petty thieves, according to Arthur. Twenty years old with brown hair and grey eyes, Yeomans had been a shoemaker in England, where he had a previous conviction, and was transported for stealing lead. Surprisingly, the first entry on his conduct record seems to relate to good conduct: soon after his arrival, on behalf of his master he forcibly prevented cattle from being impounded as payment for a debt. (If cattle were impounded

---

The Hobart Town Gazette *of February 1838 announced the date on which certain convicts could obtain their certificates of freedom. The name of the ship on which the convict had been transported to the colony was always coupled with his or her name.*

unlawfully, the owner could lawfully rescue them.) From then on it was downhill all the way for Yeomans.[15]

He spent time in chain-gangs and the public works until April 1833, when he stole leather and was transported for the first time to Port Arthur. How he happened to be having breakfast at the Swan Hotel at Bagdad, about 29 kilometres north of Hobart, in February 1838, without any money and with a fictitious cheque in his pocket, is a mystery, because his certificate of freedom was not due until March. Unluckily for Yeomans, the escapade earnt him hard labour in the Bridgewater chain-gang not far from Hobart, and he did not become free by servitude until October the following year.

When he achieved his freedom, it was brief because he was caught thieving and sentenced again to Port Arthur, but in 1844 he was transferred to Norfolk Island, a penal settlement of misery and depravity off the central coast of New South Wales. In 1855, he was returned to Port Arthur aboard the *Lady Franklin*. From some time in 1855 until 1857, while working at Snug near Hobart, Yeomans's record was apparently unblemished and he was courting Jane Ross, whom he planned to marry. One day he accused her of drinking—although he was tipsy himself—grabbed her by the hair, said ' "You b—— wretch, I'll be hung for you" ', and stabbed her with his shoemaker's knife. When a witness screamed ' "Murder!" ', Yeomans told her to stand back or he would 'serve her the same', while Jane Ross cried, ' "Catch hold of me or else I shall drop".' Ross survived to give evidence at Yeomans's trial in October 1857, at which he was sentenced to death. The sentence was commuted to life imprisonment at Port Arthur.[16] Although he had no previous record of violence at the settle-

William Yeomans, who circulated among various classes of convict discipline until 1833, when he was sent to Port Arthur. He was transported there three more times and spent nearly thirty years at the settlement and eleven at Norfolk Island.

ment, during the next twenty years he threatened another prisoner with bodily harm, and assaulted the head keeper of the separate prison, in which he was often incarcerated.

Long after the assignment system ceased in 1838 and was replaced by the probation system in the early 1840s, long after transportation came to an end in 1853, Yeomans was serving time at Port Arthur. He saw the settlement grow from a collection of wooden huts into a large town with imposing buildings, then become a white elephant too costly for the government to maintain. When the settlement closed in 1877, Yeomans was sixty-seven years old and his back was striped with the marks of 470 lashes—247 of them inflicted at Port Arthur between 1833 and 1836—and he had spent years in chain-gangs, and in solitary confinement. With other prisoners he was transferred to the Campbell Street Gaol in Hobart, where he probably spent his time breaking stones and picking oakum for mat-making.[17]

Had William Yeomans restrained himself from thieving, in 1835 he might have been in assignment instead of at Port Arthur, like Henry Tingley, who was working on an isolated farm on the east coast, where he was thankful to have a good master. Writing to his parents that year, Tingley thanked God for having plenty to eat and drink and adequate clothing:

All a man has got to mind is to keep a still tongue in his head, and do his master's duty, and then he is looked upon as if he were at home; but if he don't he may as well be hung at once, for they would take you to the magistrates and get 100 of lashes, and then get sent to a place called Port Arthur to work in irons for two or three years, and then he is disliked by every one.[18]

Tingley was well aware of the punishment that might have been his at the settlement, which was beginning to strike terror into the hearts of all convicts in Tasmania. As early as 1834, Port Arthur was succeeding beyond all Arthur's expectations for it and he felt sure it might supersede all the penal settlements of New South Wales.[19]

3 Absolute Powers

Into this changing scene at Port Arthur came 33-year-old Captain Charles O'Hara Booth of the 21st Fusiliers. He arrived at Hobart on the convict transport *Georgiana* on 2 February 1833, waited upon Lieut.-Governor Arthur, and then strolled about the town, which he assessed as 'a place that evidently will be before long of considerable size and consequence'. Booth was from Basingstoke in Hampshire. His parents, Richard and Mary Booth, had sent him to an uncle in India when he was fifteen years old, and a year later in 1816 he became an ensign in the 53rd Regiment at Madras. After applying for a commission in the 21st Fusiliers in 1830, Booth was promoted to the rank of captain and two years later he received an unwelcome and unexpected communication about his embarkation for Australia.[1]

Shortly after Booth's arrival in Hobart, his detachment disembarked to the rousing cheers of the crew of the *Georgiana* and, as he noted in his journal, 'with the compliment of a Salute from the Vessel'. Within the next few days he dined at Government House and took note of one of Arthur's pretty daughters, learnt of his appointment as commandant of Port Arthur, and in preparation for the post he became a magistrate, a justice of the peace and a coroner. Like his predecessors Russell, Mahon and Gibbons, Booth had no previous experience of command-

Captain Charles O'Hara Booth of the 21st Fusiliers, who was commandant of Port Arthur, and also in charge of Point Puer settlement for boy convicts, from 1833 to 1844. He had a profound influence on the formative years of both settlements and Tasman Peninsula generally.

ing a penal settlement and his first contact with convicts was probably during the voyage to Tasmania.

Soon he embarked on the *Tamar* for the settlement, accompanied by George Robinson, known as 'the Conciliator' for his work among the Aborigines, George's son Charles, two Aborigines, twenty-five prisoners (including a clergyman, Michael McDonagh, and a Bengal merchant, Duncan McCoy) and soldiers with their wives and children.[2] As the ship sailed into the bay at Port Arthur and Booth saw the little settlement for the first time, he concluded that he had 'a very snug (though responsible) berth'.[3]

Commandant Booth had barely had time to settle in to his cottage and assess the settlement when the *Isabella* arrived with Dr John Russell, who had returned to become acting commandant and to deliver a message to Booth from Arthur. Rather nervous of his call to Hobart, where he would be expected to give his opinions about the discipline and management of the settlement, Booth spent several days 'up to my eyes in business' with Arthur. Within hours of Booth's return to Port Arthur, the prisoners rebelled and threw pieces of brick at the Superintendent of Convicts, William Cart, a recently appointed free man whom they had refused to obey. In his inimitable style, Booth wrote in his journal that with 'an annihilating countenance' he raised his 'stentorian voice' and made the prisoners quake. It was not, he decided, 'quite so easy a Penal Settlement as hitherto', and the incident must have sharpened his awareness of the rigours of the post he had.[4]

Booth soon demonstrated that there was 'no man living better qualified' for the important charge he had, and he had 'no small experience in the philosophy of the human mind, and of the springs which actuate the motions of unprincipled men'.[5] By night and by day he devoted himself to carrying out instructions for the reorganization of Port Arthur, winning the warmest approval of the local government.[6] During his management, the settlement was a place of profound misery, which carried 'the vengeance of the law to the utmost limits of human endurance', wrote John West in *The History of Tasmania* in 1852. But his management was more humane because it was equal and impartial. West believed that Booth deserved to be remembered with respect 'as an officer who took no pleasure in the sufferings he inflicted—who was as prompt to reward as to punish'.[7]

Charles O'Hara Booth was to have a profound influence on the formative years of Port Arthur, Point Puer and Eaglehawk Neck, as well as on the coal-mines punishment station (near the north-west shore of Norfolk Bay), but despite his important role in convict management and discipline, he wrote nothing on the subject. During his command from 1833 to 1844, the settlement of Port Arthur was laid out on an extensive scale, harbour reclamation was undertaken, and the building of a massive mill and granary—said to be the largest building in the colony—was begun.

An enthusiast in the art of signalling, he established the semaphore system that efficiently linked the peninsula to Hobart and could flash messages from one signal station to another in minutes. Perhaps Booth's best-known innovation was Australia's first railway, propelled by convicts from Norfolk Bay to Long Bay near Port Arthur, and a brilliant example of his talent for organization and efficiency. The railway transported stores, passengers, and even large boats along about 8 kilometres of wooden tracks.

The new regulations gave the commandant absolute powers on Tasman Peninsula and he was answerable only to the government. As a magistrate, Booth, like his predecessors, had to ensure that trial and punishment followed the offence as quickly as possible, so that crime and its consequences would be associated in the prisoner's mind with cause and effect. Like other magistrates of the time, he ordered punishment summarily, without recourse to a court of law.[8] According to Booth, some 'nobs', including the Chief Justice, Sir John Pedder, were rather astonished at the summary system at Port Arthur when they visited the settlement in 1833, despite the regulations for the settlement having been published in the *Hobart Town Almanack* that year.[9]

The regulations stated that the commandant had to know the men brought before him so he could assign the punishment best suited to the constitution of each man's mind. He was required to admonish the prisoner and to explain to him the reason for the punishment, which was to 'inflict the requisite amount of pain or misery within the shortest period of time'. He was also to remember that ordering 'uncertain or imperfect' punishment would cause repetition of offences, increase the need to punish and be 'cruelty rather than clemency'. Flagellation was to be ordered whenever it was 'impossible to punish effectually through the mind' and was to be applied in the surgeon's presence, as was usual.

In November 1833, Booth had had six months in which to apply the new regulations and make his mark on Port Arthur. That month, the missionaries, James Backhouse and George Washington Walker, visited the settlement again to minister to the prisoners and to report on Port Arthur to the lieut.-governor, who valued the Quakers' opinions highly. The young commandant 'danced them through the Settlement', as he wrote in his journal, and the missionaries had long and satisfactory conversations with him. Backhouse and Walker knew that the government was 'more than ever desirous to make this penal settlement one of extreme severity, and most irksome restraint, depriving [the prisoners] of every indulgence, and even comfort, beyond what is merely essential to health, and enforcing the most persevering drudgery.'[10]

The missionaries came to the conclusion that while Booth had already established 'a more strict discipline' than his predecessors (and in some respects than that of Macquarie Harbour—tobacco was banned, for example), 'the punishment ... consists in its restraint, rather than in any excessive degree of labour'.[11] It was Walker's belief that the harsh discipline would be no more successful than it had been at the west coast settlement, which the missionaries knew well, but in Port Arthur's favour was 'a door open to the deserving'.[12]

One morning in April 1834, a constable hurried in to Booth to announce the arrival of the *Isabella* with Lieut.-Governor Arthur and party, which included his two little sons. Booth rode off to meet his unexpected visitors at Norfolk Bay, where they had disembarked to avoid the longer journey around the south of Tasman Peninsula, 'made my Bow and entered on topics of duty'. After the children—probably Sigismund, nearly six years old, and John, aged three—had been left with one of the families at Port Arthur, Arthur inspected the settlement and the 'lions' (prisoners), the newly established settlement for convict boys at Point Puer across the bay, and the nearby coal mines worked by Port Arthur convicts.[13]

It was Arthur's second inspection of the settlement—the first since it had been raised in status—and he expressed his satisfaction in a very flattering manner to Booth. Ever vigilant, Arthur noticed that the convicts' hair was not cut as close as it should have been and he wanted them to bathe more frequently. More importantly, he decided that 'the worst disposed Convicts shall never be left one moment unobserved by Convicts less evil inclined, by which means although bad thoughts cannot be prevented, at least bad actions will be checked'. This system of espionage would be one of the most efficient punishments as well as one of the best checks to crime. Although 'every honourable mind' would object to such a practice, the objection could not apply to Port Arthur, 'where the worst men are congregated and against whose malicious

Elizabeth Charlotte, Commandant Booth's wife. Their daughter, Amelia Patricia, was born at the settlement.

plots we must make common cause'.[14]

Perhaps Arthur's requirement that the worst should always be observed by the better-behaved was interpreted by Booth as sanction for having flagellation carried out in front of the assembled prisoners. After another visit to the settlement, some six months after Arthur's, Backhouse and Walker reported to Arthur that the practice hardened the prisoners' minds and lessened their dread of the punishment. And it was risky:

it has an exasperating effect upon bystanders; and we think, a designing man of desperate character who might be subjected to it, would not find much difficulty in throwing the Settlement into a state of insubordination, in spite of the military Guards; the Prisoners present at these times being between six and seven hundred and the Guard but forty in number.[15]

In response to the criticism, Booth agreed that public punishment had a hardening effect, but the practice had seldom occurred and he feared there was some misconception about it. According to the regulations, he had punishment carried out without delay, but on one occasion a group of desperate runaways had been caught together. Their floggings were delayed until all the prisoners were assembled, and Booth addressed them all on 'the perfect inability' of escaping and the severity of the punishment that befell anyone who ignored his advice. In two or three other cases, the offenders had been flogged in front of other members of their gang only.[16]

Even though conditions were becoming grim, until the number of solitary cells were increased many small offences were overlooked as being too insignificant to warrant a term in the chain-gang or flagellation. But after Booth had been at Port Arthur for two years, the most trifling instance of misconduct or breach of regulations came to be recorded as an offence. By then the increase in cells enabled certain men to be sentenced to solitary confinement on bread and water instead of a flogging, which was what Arthur had hoped for in 1830. In 1833, the average number of lashes was fifty, but between 1835 and 1836 the average decreased from thirty-six to twenty-seven. The authorities were pleased with the decrease, because the conduct of convicts in other parts of the colony depended on the success of Port Arthur, and it was proving to be successful without excessive flogging.[17]

Over the next decade, however, sentences of a hundred lashes would not be uncommon at Port Arthur, even though Booth was said to loathe the lash, and it was used freely at the settlement's punishment station, the coal mines, on Norfolk Bay, a place which some convicts dreaded more than Port Arthur. Booth's dislike of flagellation was recorded by Lempriere in *The Penal Settlements of Van Diemen's Land*: 'We should be guilty of an act of injustice to . . . Captain Booth, did we not here state that . . . he detests the use of [the lash], and it is with regret, when he is compelled by the necessity of maintaining strict discipline, that he causes corporal punishment to be inflicted'.

Booth came to believe that 'nothing but the severest measures can operate on the minds of these men with good effect'. Arthur had the utmost confidence in him and had given him approval to do whatever he believed was necessary to attain 'perfect *Security* and *Discipline*' at Port Arthur, yet when Booth had not been there long and wanted to increase the penalties for absconding, he hesitated, and referred the matter to his superiors. However, there was no objection to his sentencing escapees to flogging as well as to a term in leg-irons.[18] Nor were there objections to an innovative, if not unique, punishment he introduced some time in the late 1830s: a heavy log of wood tied to a man's leg-irons which he slowly dragged after him everywhere he went. Another innovation were stalls, like kennels, in which prisoners were chained while they stood before a bench and broke stones with a hammer.

Absconding continued to be a serious crime, said to be encouraged by Booth's rigorous discipline. In 1834, for instance, three prisoners bolted because he had put a stop to trafficking and luxuries, such as tobacco. (He also banned fishing, but relented on Christmas Eve in 1833 and allowed the men to stop work early and fish for the following day's dinner.)[19] Nevertheless, he celebrated his first anniversary at Port Arthur feeling rather fortunate that no prisoners had escaped from the peninsula, thanks to his personal vigilance and an efficient detachment of military.

To the commandant of a penal settlement, personal danger was always at hand. Although the convict, Linus Miller, called Booth 'an excellent man' in his *Notes of an Exile*, and the historian, John West, had never heard a prisoner speak with reproach of Booth, who was 'detested only as the personification of unimpassioned severity', the commandant himself described in his journal how a man 'declared he would have my life' if sentenced to corporal punishment.

On one occasion, one of a gang of forty prisoners warned Booth of a plot to kill him. The commandant walked straight into the middle of the gang and told the ringleader he would have been a dead man before he could have approached Booth, because 'I should not have hesitated to shoot you'. Booth was invariably armed with pistols.[20] In contrast, in April 1834, Commandant Booth was touched by the concern the prisoners showed when he was delayed from returning to Port Arthur from a tour of inspection and three search parties were sent out for him. In his journal he wrote: 'it afforded me very infinite pleasure to see the interest that our situation had excited—even to the most depraved Prisoners'. If he was also astonished at this response, he did not say so.

Restlessly energetic, Booth walked or rode everywhere over his domain, sometimes alone, sometimes accompanied by other staff. He made frequent inspections, searched for escapees, climbed mountains in search of sites for signal stations as part of

the semaphore system on the peninsula, and enjoyed hunting and shooting. He came to know the rugged peninsula well, yet he was never a good bushman. In 1838, while on his way to Norfolk Bay to investigate a report of a shipwreck, he was lost in the bush for four days and a dramatic search ensued. The Commissariat Officer, Thomas Lempriere, set off from Port Arthur with two soldiers and the commandant's boat and convict crew to join a party of settlers who had already begun the search.

Booth had been accompanied by a coxswain, Turner, a vindictive character whom he had recently sentenced to fifty lashes for misconduct. After Turner became separated from Booth, he met up with the searchers, who feared the convict had deliberately left the commandant to perish in the bush. Lempriere interrogated Turner, but he was reluctant to answer questions and was not at all sympathetic to Booth's plight. When Turner merely said, ' "Worse accidents have happened at sea" ', Lempriere thought the soldiers 'would have shot the poor fellow on the spot, so convinced were they that he had made away with their beloved officer'. Turner's story was that he had stopped to remove a thorn in his foot, while Booth continued, and they lost sight of each other.[21]

News of the search reached Government House during a ball being held by the Lieut.-Governor, Sir John Franklin, and Lady Franklin, who wrote: 'Great was the consternation . . . not only on account of the extraordinary merit of Capt. Booth, but on account of the probability of the convicts rising *en masse* under such favourable circumstances'. Reinforcements were despatched to Port Arthur on the *Eliza*, but by the time the

A late nineteenth-century drawing of the commandant's house at Port Arthur, after it had been extended and improved by the addition of an impressive entrance. When Booth arrived it was a mere cottage. Sometimes he had to move out when official visitors such as the lieut.-governor arrived.

soldiers reached the settlement, Booth had been found, desperately ill, with his faithful kangaroo dogs, Daphne, Sandy and Young Spring by his side. He had been too weak and faint to reply to the cooees and the sound of bugles, while the trigger on one of his pistols had broken and the other had become wet through.[22] His plight worsened when his well-meaning rescuers lit a fire and moved him too close to it, causing excruciating agony to his frost-bitten feet.[23]

The searchers took Booth back to Port Arthur, where, again, he was touched by the response of the prisoners: 'The good feeling . . . evidenced by the Prisoners and wretched little Boys at Point Puer also speaks greatly in behalf of their still possessing some latent sparks of good—which if only worked on firmly and rigidly yet kindly—much good—it is to be hoped, may be done.' This was one of the rare occasions on which his feelings about the prisoners emerged in the journal.[24]

Like Arthur, the Franklins thought highly of Booth, who was, wrote Lady Franklin, never again to venture into the bush alone: 'for what with his daring fearless nature, and his absence of mind, which is always at work upon the interests of the settlement, (wherever he may be in the body) this is the third or fourth time the same accident has happened to him'.[25] Sir John Franklin was to write later that there was no officer or friend in the colony whose services and character he valued more. 'I am fully aware of the vast importance and great responsibility of the trust reposed in you, and that you fulfill its duties with a judgment, energy, discretion and zeal which few could exercise in the like manner and none exceed.'[26]

During his term as commandant from 1833 until 1844, Booth was homesick for England, considered going on the land and once threatened to resign his post over a minor matter, but the ordeal in the bush was the cause of his premature departure from Port Arthur. An active man with great powers of endurance, he lost his previous vigour. He sold out from the army in 1839, remaining at the settlement as the civil, not army, commandant at the government's request. After the introduction of the probation system to the colony in the early 1840s, his responsibilities were restricted to Port Arthur and Point Puer, the constables and semaphore signalmen, with visits of inspection to other stations on the peninsula. In 1844, he took a less demanding post as the superintendent of the Queen's Orphan School near Hobart. He died at the age of fifty, in August 1851, at his home Stoke at New Town.[27]

In 1838, Booth had married a widow, Elizabeth Eagle, who had one child, and the following year their daughter, Amelia Patricia, was born at Port Arthur. After her husband's death, Mrs Booth returned to England in 1852 and attempted to obtain a pension to support herself and the children. Booth's salary had been £300 a year at Port Arthur, increasing to £500 shortly before he resigned, and at the Queen's Orphan School he received, in addition to a salary, a pension of £100 a year. In support of Mrs Booth's petition, testimonials emphasized that Booth's ordeal in the bush had led to his premature death, and he had been unable to provide for his family because his position at Port Arthur had made heavy demands on his salary.[28]

At the settlement, Booth had been expected to accommodate visitors, who ranged from strangers to the governor and other officials. Not until 1853 was Government Cottage built, near the church, to accommodate visitors and relieve the strain on the commandant's purse-strings. From the late 1830s, the authorities apparently encouraged visitors to inspect Port Arthur and it became a showplace for the government. According to Sir John Franklin, the visits 'tend to materially improve the character of the settlement, and in many other ways to be productive of real advantage'.

4 Growth and Expansion

By the late 1830s, Port Arthur was beginning to resemble a substantial town and bore little resemblance to its former shanty-like appearance. Although there were still a number of timber buildings, several fine stone or brick structures had been added to the settlement, giving it a look of permanence. A military air pervaded Port Arthur and cries of 'Who goes there?' and 'All's well' were heard from the military, whose red coats contrasted with the coarse yellow, yellow and black, or grey clothing of the prisoners. Deep green Tasmanian ivy creeping up some of the buildings stood out against the dazzling whitewash of the sombre wooden structures and the mellowness of stone. From the bay or from the Eaglehawk Neck road, the view that unfolded was attractive, if not striking, but the prospect of life at Port Arthur must have filled the hearts of convicts with dread as their ships dropped anchor in the bay.

Set apart slightly from the other buildings and situated in the centre of an impressive garden near the water's edge was the commandant's house, which was surrounded by fruit trees and berries and almost every plant to be found in an English garden. Originally a small brick cottage, it had been extended to include a verandah enclosed by venetian blind windows. The more modest houses of the staff were built in rows on a slope, and

This is the earliest known view of Port Arthur and was drawn in 1839 when the French ship, L'Artemise, *was in port. The captain treated the settlement's staff to 'an elegant Tiffin and a set of quadrilles'. A rare view of Point Puer is in the background.*

between them were 'little footpath terraces one above the other on the bank'. As only human labour was permitted on the settlement at this time, roads were not required for horse-drawn vehicles, although the paths were wide enough to accommodate the three-wheeled carts in which convicts trundled firewood and water to the houses. Further colour was added to the settlement on an area set aside for staff gardens—vegetables, plums, pears, figs, peaches, apples, cherries, cucumbers, melons and berry fruits were grown.[1]

On a hill behind the commandant's house was the semaphore, which was erected on a trunk of a tree as lofty as the mast of a large ship and formed a picturesque and prominent feature of Port Arthur. Within minutes, many sentences, questions, answers and orders could be signalled between other signal posts on the peninsula and Hobart. At first the semaphore arms had been operated by ropes and block and tackle, but later the ropes, which rotted, were replaced by an improved and faster system of chains. Signals were sent by moving the arms, which represented numbers, and hundreds of sentences, questions, answers, directions and orders could be transmitted. Each letter of the alphabet had a separate number so that if any word was not represented by a number in the established code, it could be spelt out. There were several smaller semaphores at the settlement for local use.[2]

As prominent but more pleasing aesthetically was the large and imposing freestone church, 'a beautiful, spacious, hewn-stone edifice, cruciform in shape, with pinnacled tower and gables'.[3] In 1834, shortly after Booth received instructions to

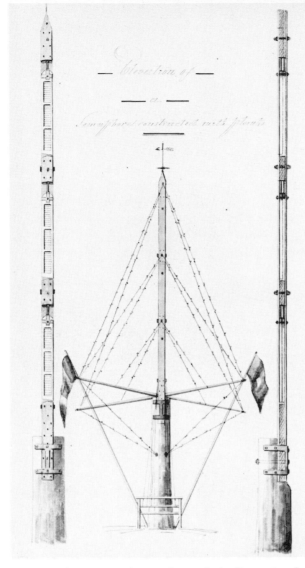

Elevation of

Semaphore constructed with ...

A drawing from Commandant Booth's own book of instructions for the use of the semaphore signal system. Messages could be relayed from station to station within minutes.

A rare front view of the tower and spire of the Port Arthur church, which faced an avenue of trees. The first service was held in 1837. In about 1854, a new clock was fixed in the tower, which had a spiral staircase. At this time the interior was being improved because it had become damp, dirty and mildewed.

Opposite:
'The Penal Settlement of Port Arthur, January 1844', a watercolour by E. A. Porcher, a member of a coastal surveying expedition.

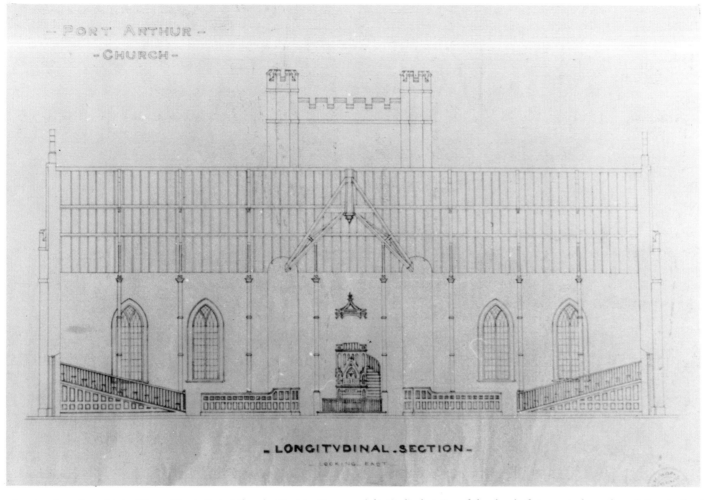

PORT ARTHUR

CHURCH

_ LONGITVDINAL . SECTION _

LOOKING EAST

A watercolour of convicts in Champ Street, Port Arthur, by Captain Owen Stanley, who described them as 'a most miserable sight'. When he visited the settlement between December 1840 and January 1841, the spire had not been added to the church, at right.

A longitudinal section of the church, facing east, shows the pulpit and other fittings made by Point Puer boy convicts.

build a chapel, Lempriere, who was an enthusiastic amateur artist, wrote in his diary of completing two plans for 'a church for our small town', and the following year he was 'busy in drawing an elevation for our new church'. Thomas Lempriere made no claim for designing the building, though it is possible that his plans contributed to its design. The preliminary church plans that have survived were drawn in 1836 by a convict architect, Henry Laing, who was first sent to Port Arthur in 1834 and again in 1836. During four years on Tasman Peninsula, Laing was responsible for drawings, plans and estimates for all the buildings erected while he was at Port Arthur, including the mill and granary.[4] The tall main spire of the church was not included on Laing's 1836 drawing and it was added to the tower some time between January 1841 and late in 1842. Built of pine, the spire was painted a stone colour, and while wet it was sifted over with powdered stone to give it a look of authenticity.[5] The tower beneath the spire had a peal of eight bells and a small window at the top of the tower was replaced with a clock in 1855.

If there have been doubts about the identity of the architect of the church, there are none about that of the workers who cut the stone for the church and made most of its fittings. The masons and carpenters were boy convicts from Point Puer who were being trained in trades to fit them for life in the colony after their release. Despite the authorities' resolve to separate the boys from the men, some of them were brought across the bay to Port Arthur, where they learnt stonecutting, while in the Point Puer workshops the boy carpenters prepared the simple but neat fittings for the building's interior.[6]

On 25 April 1836, the foundation stone of the church was laid by Lieut.-Governor Arthur, who gave 'an appropriate but neat address' for the occasion. Fifteen months later, in July, the first service was held in the bitterly cold building, which was unfinished and had only one glazed window. About a thousand people could be seated—the free in high, dark-coloured pews and the convicts on wooden benches—and the seating capacity could be extended by adding galleries, although this was never necessary. Around one pew was 'the old-fashioned English curtain, so that the mighty one within might pray or sleep without intrusion', and the pulpit was lofty and fortress-like. By the mid 1840s the interior of this splendid church had become 'dirty, damp and mildewed'.[7]

Although Booth had been instructed to avoid the slightest degree of ornamentation on any of the buildings, there was decoration in abundance, giving the court and the military barracks within it a novel appearance for Tasmania, according to Lempriere. Another author thought the military barracks had a very quaint style more suited to 'the primaeval ages' than a penal settlement. A third considered that the architect of the settlement must have been of 'a cheery and playful mind', because almost every building had 'a profusion of little turrets, castellated copings, sham machicolations and pie-crust battlements' that reminded him of an Isle of Wight villa![8]

The military barracks was situated in the centre of a court or quadrangle, the walls at the rear and sides being studded with square turrets. At the rear of the court was a turret large enough for a sentry to 'command the approaches in that direction as well as to protect the powder magazine, a small building securely built, surmounted with a fence'. In front of the court was the stone guard tower, built in 1835 from stone cut by Point Puer boys. In his *Penal Settlements of Van Diemen's Land*, Lempriere described the tower:

The front of the Barrack Yard is guarded by a circular tower, through which a passage leads by a double flight of steps to the Guard House on its base story. In the passage are two doors, one leading to two cells, in which are kept some large blunderbusses ready for action; the other by a winding staircase reaching to the summit on which is placed a staff. On Sunday or when a person of consequence is at the Settlement or when a vessel enters or leaves the harbour, a Union Jack is hoisted on the staff. Two small towers, embattled in the same way as the large one, occupy the right and left angles of the Court.

The contrast between the few, fine, permanent stone structures and the inadequate temporary accommodation for prisoners was marked.

In 1832, Gibbons had found the prisoners' huts impossible to keep orderly and clean, and the men not only slept in them but had to cook and eat their meals in them as well. Arthur had agreed with him that proper barracks were needed, but several decades would pass before the accommodation was improved.[9]

In the meantime, soon after his arrival, Booth wrote hopefully to his superiors of his plans for a three-storey brick penitentiary with rubble masonry foundations, which he thought could include 237 separate cells with two exercise yards, as well as huts for 450 men grouped around a general muster ground.[10] However, he was too optimistic. In November 1833, the prisoners were still in bark huts, and a year later, the huts, although clean and wholesome, were dilapidated.

The paling stockade was to be enlarged to make space for new huts and Arthur wanted them to be substantial, weather-tight and airy, although any other comfort would be objectionable for convicts, even if it could be achieved cheaply. As well, a large number of solitary cells would be built simply and inexpensively, as 'dismal abodes' for the most vicious characters, who would be locked in them after their day's work was done. In contrast to these cells, there would be a 'warm and cheerful' schoolroom for illiterate and semi-literate prisoners, which would be built first, and be the only hut with any semblance of comfort. The contrast between the schoolroom and the cells was intended to have a beneficial effect on those whose feelings 'are not totally destroyed', and would encourage the men in the cells to reform in order to enjoy the advantages of the schoolroom.[11]

Perhaps Booth's added responsibilities contributed to slowing the building programme, because late in 1833 he had to turn his attention to establishing the experimental settlement for boys at Point Puer, which he nurtured in its formative years, as he did Port Arthur and other convict stations on the peninsula. Yet another contribution to the delay must have been the lack of prisoners qualified to undertake building, which was often delayed for that reason throughout the colony. In fact, Arthur had written to Governor Richard Bourke in Sydney to ask for some labourers, especially carpenters and masons, to enable him to erect a large substantial gaol on the peninsula. Whatever the cause of the delay, at the end of 1834 the new penitentiary being constructed consisted merely of small huts like the old ones and a range of eighty cells.[12]

On a dark, wet night in 1836, the penitentiary seemed dismal and forbidding to the *Hobart Town Almanack*:

The barracks were temporary buildings composed of logs, and for the most part, covered with bark ... the rain had converted [the soil] into mud, and stepping stones and thin slabs of wood had been laid ... from door to door. The darkness ... prevented us of availing ourselves of the aid. ... At one time we were up to the ankles in mud, and at another, slipping the foot from the edge into a puddle. ... A lane or passage extended on all sides round the barracks, and a lamp being placed at each corner the soldiers who walk along see every person who moves out of his quarters at night or attempts to escape, a luminous lamp being placed at every corner. A solemn silence pervaded the whole, interrupted only by the solitary tread of the sentinels.

At this time the huts were often whitewashed with lime to give them a clean, wholesome appearance, which tended to impress visitors, according to Lempriere. Within the stockade were several separate yards. In one, for example, there were huts for certain convict overseers, boats' crew, watchmen, singers in the church choir, men on probation, and boys temporarily at the settlement. About thirty men slept in each

hut, although the number varied somewhat, and at the end of each one the overseers slept, positioned so that they could observe the men with the aid of a lamp kept burning through the night. Each bunk was partitioned off from the other, an arrangement that was considered to be conducive to cleanliness and a prevention against immorality.[13]

Some of the other buildings at the settlement included a former gaol, on which had been painted a number of lancet-shaped false windows to relieve its severity, a commissariat store (for the prisoners' food and supplies), a cook-house and a bakehouse, workshops, a lumber yard, sawpits and, nearby, a shipbuilding yard. One of the finest buildings, erected in 1842, was the hospital, situated on the hill overlooking the settlement—a fine brick structure with a stone facade, containing four wards with about eighteen beds in each. Though the wards had lofty ceilings they were poorly ventilated. There was also a well-arranged surgery, a dissecting-room for the dead, and a kitchen.[14]

In the mid 1830s, Booth's ingenious plan for a primitive, convict-propelled railway between Norfolk Bay near Eagle-hawk Neck and Long Bay near Port Arthur provoked sneers from some colonists who predicted its failure. But the railway succeeded and it proved to be a valuable, though peculiar, asset to Tasman Peninsula for many years, because it shortened the route between Port Arthur and Hobart by avoiding the longer sea voyage around the south of the peninsula. Until the railway

A photograph of Port Arthur before it was closed in 1877. The decrepit old penitentiary is in the foreground at right. The four-storey mill and granary, converted to a penitentiary in 1857, is at left.

The brick hospital with stone facade was built in 1842. It was badly damaged by fire in 1895, restored, and burnt beyond repair in another fire in 1897. This photograph may have been taken just after the restoration.

was built in about 1836, transporting stores to stations such as the coal mines on the western shore of Norfolk Bay or to the Neck was extremely slow, as they were carried on the backs of convicts along rough bush paths from Port Arthur, or by boat.[15]

When the railway was established, a line of trees was marked out along the intended route, the trees were felled and bridges were built over creeks and deep hollows on the route. The chosen route had as few hills as possible, to avoid time-consuming excavations; nevertheless, it was far from flat. Along the route, logs of wood 2 metres long were spaced about 30 centimetres apart as sleepers, and to these were nailed wooden rails about 15 centimetres in breadth and 6 centimetres thick. The space between the sleepers was filled up with sand and clay.[16]

The carriages or waggons were 'very low, double seated, with four very small cast iron wheels, the same used in quarries' in England. The prisoners pushed the carriages by seizing bars at the front and the rear, jumping aboard while going downhill, when the speed was said to be up to 48 kilometres an hour.[17] In *Our Antipodes*, Colonel Godfrey Mundy, with his discerning eye and lively pen, wrote: 'after pushing with great toil up a considerable plane, [the convicts] reached the top of a long descent, when, getting up their steam, down they rattled at tremendous speed—tremendous, at least, to lady-like nerves— the chains around their ankles chinking and clanking as they trotted along'. Downhill, 'the runners jumped upon the side of the trucks in a rather unpleasant proximity with the passengers, and away we all went, bondsmen and freemen, jolting and swaying in a manner that smacked somewhat too much of "the d——l take the hindmost"—although a man sitting behind contrived, more or less, to lock a wheel with a wooden crowbar when the descent became so rapid as to call for remonstrance'.

Colonel Godfrey Mundy's view of the convict-propelled railway, which he rode on in 1851.

This light-hearted account belies Mundy's feelings for the plight of the convicts. He was moved to see them 'terribly jaded, running down with sweat, and I saw one of them continually trying to shift his irons from a galled spot on his ankle'. Once the journey halted so that the prisoners could eat because they had had nothing for twelve hours. Like Mundy, passengers on the railway were usually appalled by the convict-propelled railway, while being intrigued by the method of transport. A settler, David Burn, after remarking that it 'jars harshly against the feelings to behold man, as it were, lowered to the standards of the brute', reminded himself and his readers of free British labourers—coal-heavers, bargemen, dockmen and the like—whose drudgery was equal to that of the railwaymen at Tasman Peninsula.

In the 1830s, Australia had no railways, and Britain's were in their infancy, passenger trains travelling at about 24 to 32 kilometres an hour, while meetings were held to stress that 16 kilometres an hour was an entirely adequate speed. Many colonists had never seen a railway, let alone had a ride on one, and the speed achieved at times on the Port Arthur railway must have terrified some of its passengers. During a ride in 1838, Lady Franklin coolly noted the railway's statistics, but Booth in his diary entry for the day, wrote that the ladies were 'a little frightened' because the waggons went through to Long Bay at 'a posting rate'.

Another passenger, Francis J. Cockburn, in his *Letters from the Southern Hemisphere*, described his experience:

Nothing on earth could stop you. You come to a curve, and lest the car should fly off, the two men on the one side, keeping only one foot on the car, lean out as far as possible to 'carry her round'. If one of these men chose simply to sit down, the chances are the car would fly off, and if it went against one of the numerous trees which grow along the line your head would suffer, I fancy.

As we were going down a gentle descent on our return, I asked a Mr Allen of the Engineers, who was beside me, what pace we were going,

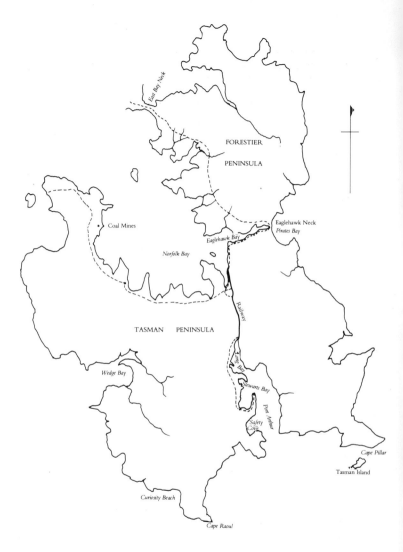

A map of Tasman Peninsula showing Port Arthur, Eaglehawk Neck, Eaglehawk Bay, the railway between Norfolk Bay and Long Bay, and also the coal mines.

and before he had time to reply there was a shock and a whirr, and we were off the line. Luckily no damage was done, and we went on again immediately. We were then going about eighteen miles an hour.

In April 1833, Commandant Booth 'got a spill' from a waggon, to the amusement of a fellow officer, and came to no harm, but others were not so fortunate. Some years later in 1843 the Colonial Secretary, James Bicheno, received 'tremendous concussion'. Another public official landed in a ditch and was set on his feet by the convict railwaymen, who 'amid a thousand expressions of contrition', brushed the dirt from his clothes and, at the same time, removed his watch and purse.[18]

The railway became the model for at least two others, at Ralph Bay Neck and East Bay Neck. In *Varieties of Vice-regal Life*, the Lieut.-Governor, Sir William Denison, described a visit to Tasman Peninsula in 1847 during his first year of office, when he went by boat down the Derwent River and crossed Ralph Bay Neck on the railway, which had been constructed by Port Arthur convicts:

there is a railway running across the neck, and a station with some convicts, who are employed in pushing the carriages across. The water is very shallow, and the railway runs out a great distance [into it]. When we arrived, we saw the carriages waiting for us; and when I say 'carriages', I mean a sort of small waggon. . . . I must say that my feelings at seeing myself seated, and pushed along by these miserable convicts, were not very pleasant. It was painful to see them in the condition of slaves, which, in fact, they are, waiting for me up to their knees in water.

In the late 1830s, the authorities became aware of the financial losses being incurred by shipping flour to Port Arthur from Hobart. Annually, settlers from various parts of the colony sent shiploads of wheat to the town, running the risk of losing the grain during a shipwreck en route. Several vessels had been wrecked in 1838. Further financial loss occurred while the grain was stored in Hobart and then shipped as flour to the settlement. However, if the prisoners could raise grain on the peninsula and grind it there, they could contribute to their own support.

A Board of Enquiry, appointed in 1838, concluded that wheat cultivated on the peninsula would be a security risk because it would enable absconders to subsist, and they would be further aided by the buildings necessary for such an extended system of agriculture. Although only the continued cultivation of vegetables was recommended, as necessary for the prisoners' health, soon wheat was cultivated, but never on a large scale.[19]

It was decided, however, to build a flour mill and granary at Port Arthur where wheat would be ground and stored. The building, designed by Henry Laing, is Port Arthur's largest. But not until February 1843 was the laying of the foundations begun, under the supervision of a millwright and engineer, Alexander Clark, who also built the mill-race and installed the machinery. From the start, Clark was faced with many frustrations, largely caused by convict labourers and overseers, building on reclaimed land and using poor quality bricks. While laying the foundations with 'good large heavy hard stones', on a natural beach, the prisoners had great difficulty in keeping out the sea water.[20]

Over the next two years, the millwright often complained bitterly of tardy progress, and at one stage he was left with only one bricklayer to work on a building that was to be four storeys high and measure 70 metres long by 11 metres wide. The lack of bricklayers was probably caused by the vigilance of the convict overseers, whom Clark described:

many of the Prisoner Constables, who go prowling about . . . never fail to pounce upon some unfortunate *Creature* who is with impunity, as far as the Constables are concerned, taken to the office and some charge of the most trifling nature (perhaps a false one) laid . . . and punishment awarded . . . almost always *Solitary* or a Sentence of *Three* or *Six Months* imposed of *hard Labour* in *Chains*, thus depriving me of the *Labourer* and in fact of many a good Workman. . . .

The flour mill and granary was powered by two water wheels and a treadwheel worked by the convicts. It has been described as 'an architectural wonder of its time'. In 1857 it was occupied as a new and splendid penitentiary and the prisoners' decrepit old huts were used for ex-convicts—elderly invalids, the destitute and the mentally ill.

Among other frustrations was the disappearance of equipment intended for Clark's use which was apparently being commandeered by officers at Port Arthur. Clark had 'almost given up all hopes of ever seeing another glazed window, or hung door on the Works, much less the Venetian Windows, of which the officers of the Commissariat have taken such an interest'. Even worse, a part of the wall of the first storey of the building gave way and had to be rebuilt. Meanwhile, some of the bricklayers and stonemasons required Clark's undivided attention and he often had to take the plumb rule from one of them and adjust the work himself.

The mill and granary had progressed amazingly when an argument between the Commandant, William Thomas Napier Champ, who had succeeded Booth in 1844, and the Roman Catholic chaplain, Mr Bond, halted work temporarily on the top floor of the building. Champ had decided that the Catholic chapel should be situated there, above the treadwheel, but the priest refused to accept this as a permanent arrangement. To Clark, it was 'a matter of perfect indifference . . . whether the space be converted into a Chapel or a Play House'.

Although the Commissariat Department was anxious to begin grinding wheat, putting the treadwheel to work was delayed from consideration for the prisoners who would be operating it. As the floor above the wheel had not been laid, the men would have been exposed to the weather and to rubble falling from above, where bricklayers and carpenters were still working. Finally, when the treadwheel performed its first revolution on 3 March 1845, no one could have been more pleased than Clark that part of the building was in use. According to him, the event 'excited unusual interest here, a large concourse of visitors was attracted . . . to witness this trial of mechanical skill'. The 'smooth, correct and steady revolution of the different parts of the Machinery . . . elicited plaudits and universal admiration'. Even the convicts—the ultimate authority—were said to admire the wheel, because it was steadier to work than its counterpart in Hobart.

In June 1845, the shingle roof was at last completed, but still the water wheels were not, and the cutting and laying of flagstones, as well as work on the wooden staircases, continued during 1846. At full production, the granary, which had four floors, held about 300 000 bushels of grain and there were two machines for dressing the flour. When all three sets of wheels were working, about 18 bushels of flour could be ground in an hour. Yet despite the time and energy involved in erecting the building, which was said to be the largest in the colony, in 1851—possibly earlier—the wheels were still. The building was in use as a mill and granary for not many more years than had been taken to erect it.[21] The reasons why this immense structure became obsolete so soon may have included the lack of water at the settlement to power the water wheels. In the 1850s, a politician, amid 'loud bursts of laughter' from his colleagues, criticized the government for building the mill at Port Arthur, where, he claimed, for nine months of the year there was not enough water to work the wheels.[22]

5 Our Penal Settlement

To most convicts the bewildering journey across unknown seas to an unknown land was the longest journey of their lives and the first and last sea voyage they would undertake. If they made another, it was likely to be the result of a sentence of transportation to Port Arthur, although there were some who managed to escape from the colony and board a ship for Victoria or farther afield. On the other hand, some convicts returned to Britain, only to commit another crime and be retransported to Australia or elsewhere, like 'a hale old man with the silver hair, and skin as dark as a mulatto's' at the Gibraltar Convict Prison in the 1870s. A veteran survivor of transportation to the Antipodes, the old man had been twice 'across the pond', first to Botany Bay and then to Port Arthur.[1]

Soon after a convict ship arrived from England and anchored in the Derwent River, a ritual was carried out to record each prisoner's description. Each one was placed in a gauge to measure height, and the colour of eyes, hair, complexion, and any identifying marks such as tattoos were noted. Many men were tattooed—marks sometimes acquired during the voyage—and if a prisoner absconded, his tattoo marks were always listed in the *Hobart Town Gazette*, with his description, as an aid to identification. James Baker, for instance, who was sent to Port Arthur in 1854, not only had the words health, love and liberty tattooed on his body, but two birds, two mermaids, a

Convicts working at Port Arthur in the mid 1840s. One man seems to be wearing his jacket back to front because the initials P. A. and his number are reversed.

man with a flag, a wreath, swords, pistols, a bottle and two glasses, a crucifix, a crown, two flags and an anchor.[2] As well as keeping descriptions, the Convict Department held up-to-date information about pardons, confessions, offences, punishments, meritorious conduct resulting in a reduced sentence, marriages, deaths. From the day of their landing until their emancipation or death, each convict was supposed to be regularly and strictly accounted for.

While the arrival of a convict ship was common enough and rarely caused a stir in Hobart, certain groups occasionally attracted a crowd of townspeople. In 1839 and 1840, residents who knew nothing of Canada and still less of Canadians, were intrigued when the Canadian exiles disembarked. They had been transported for their part in the Canadian rebellion in the 1830s. One of the exiles, William Gates, in his *Recollections of Life in Van Diemen's Land*, described the effect they had: 'Ladies from their carriages would exclaim to one another … "Why, they look like our men, don't they?" "They are white, too, and they speak just like our men!" "I would not have believed it had I not seen it." ' (Small groups of convicts also arrived from Singapore, Hong Kong, Aden and the Cape of Good Hope, and a few from India, Mauritius, Gibraltar, Bermuda and New Zealand went to Port Arthur.)

Like all newly arrived convicts, the Canadians were taken to the Hobart penitentiary, known as The Tench. It was the general depot for all prisoners on arrival, but it also received men who had been retransported to the settlement. Until a ship was ready to leave, they were locked up in a cell or dormitory, while their clothing and property were stored until their return. In 1840, Linus Miller, a 19-year-old former law student in Canada, was sentenced to Port Arthur for absconding from a road party. He spent some time in a vermin-ridden dormitory in the penitentiary. Appalled by the 'most revolting and diabolical' scenes, he slept only about two hours nightly because he was so afraid. When Miller tried to assist a battered victim who was robbed in the night, a voice whispered, ' "If you say one word about this affair, we'll cut your bloody heart out to-morrow night!" '

Nineteen-year-old Linus Miller, centre, with two other Canadian prisoners, Paul Bedford, left, and William Reynolds. Bedford was executed in London, and Miller and Reynolds were transported.

When the brig *Isabella* was ready to sail, Miller and forty-five others, all wearing leg-irons and handcuffed in pairs, boarded her. They were crowded into a small area in which few could enjoy the luxury of sitting at any one time, and those who could not sit 'were obliged to support themselves upon their feet, and lean forward . . . clinging with their manacled hands, to their companions'. As the vessel pitched and tossed during the voyage across Storm Bay and around the south of Tasman Peninsula, the men were thrown on the deck, their irons wrenching their aching limbs. 'Nearly all were sea-sick, and the deck was literally a pool of nauseous matter, produced by vomiting', wrote Miller with distaste, in *Notes of an Exile*. 'Every man was wet to the skin with it, and the stench was intolerable.' After thirty-six hours they reached Port Arthur in a thoroughly miserable state.

In 1841, another prisoner showed a lively disregard for authority during a similar journey to the settlement. He was William Derrincourt (alias Jones, alias Day), who had been transported for ten years for house-breaking and was on his way to Port Arthur as the result of assaulting a constable. In his *Old Convict Days*, he wrote:

we were put down in the hold, where there was stretched a long cable. . . . To the cable we were fettered. Passing the Iron Pot, a small island down the harbour, we all began singing, shouting and making a great noise. We were told that if we did not quieten when told we should be forced to do so. We still persisted, when two or three turns were given to the capstan, tightening the cable, and we were held up by our fettered feet, and with our heads downwards, until we promised good behaviour.

Similarly, Martin Cash, who was on board the *Tamar* in 1842, was stowed in the hold, in total darkness, his only bedding the stones the brig carried as ballast. He had been sentenced to Port Arthur for absconding and would later become one of the settlement's most notorious escapees. In *The Bushranger of Van Diemen's Land*, he gives an insight into the prisoners' arrival at

Port Arthur. After they were sent ashore in a boat, they were inspected, and each man's hair was cut short by the barber. 'He scorned the use of a comb . . . merely catching the hair with one hand and using the scissors with the other', wrote Cash. The convict clerks took the men's descriptions, and they were then marched to the stores, where the irons were removed from those not sentenced to wear them.

Each prisoner was given a suit of clothing—yellow, parti-coloured (yellow and black) or grey, depending on their classification. The suit consisted of cloth trousers, jacket and waistcoat, to be worn winter and summer. Striped shirts, a pair of ankle boots and a leather cap, which fitted the head closely and projected in four points that could be turned up or down, completed the outfit. The yellow suit had a nickname, 'canary'. The yellow and black was 'a vile, dirty, coarse, threadbare, cloth suit (no lining, no drawers) . . . called "magpie",' wrote John Mortlock in disgust in *Experiences of a Convict*, no doubt remembering the magnificent velvet-lined coat he had worn at Cambridge in England. Mortlock had been transported for

twenty-one years for attempting to murder his uncle, was first sent to Norfolk Island, and was at Port Arthur in the early 1850s.

At the hospital each man was given a physical examination, and later the regulations were read. The following thirteen sections were read to all prisoners at least once a month:

46. Every convict is to pay the most implicit obedience to the lawful commands of his superiors: if he shall consider himself aggrieved by any order, he is nevertheless to obey instantly, but may complain afterwards, if he shall think fit, to the Commandant.
47. He is on all occasions, when passing a civil or military officer, to salute in a respectful manner, by touching his cap.
48. He is at all times and in all places to conduct himself with the utmost order and regularity, and at every muster, as well as in marching to and from labour, he is to preserve the strictest silence.
49. He is not to have in his possession any article or thing whatever,

The guards at Port Arthur in the 1860s, photographed by Alfred Bock, who was in business between 1855 and about 1865 and was the first Australian-born professional photographer.

either of food, clothing, or otherwise, except such as shall have been issued to him or sanctioned by the Commandant; tobacco and all articles of luxury being especially prohibited.

50. He is on no account to absent himself from his gang, or appointed place of work, or when in barracks, to leave the yard to which he belongs, or enter any other hut than his own, without express permission.

51. He is always to appear as clean in his person and dress as circumstances will admit; he is to take care that his clothing, boots, bedding, plate, pannican and spoon are marked with his local number; and he is not to damage, wilfully, give away, lend or exchange any of these articles, on any pretence whatever.

52. Should any article issued or entrusted to him be lost or damaged, he is to report the same immediately to his overseer.

53. If in chains he is held responsible that his irons are perfect, and not ovalled, or too large.

54. He is not to perform any private work or labour whatever unless ordered to do so by his overseer, or some superior authority.

55. He is not to send or receive any letters or packages, except through the Commandant, who will exercise his discretion in opening them, and ascertaining their contents.

56. He is not to hold communication with any of the military, or with any sailor or person not belonging to the settlement, except when on duty.

57. If he have anything to represent or to complain of, he must address himself in the first instance to the superintendent [of convicts]; but he is never to address the Commandant at the time of any muster or parade.

58. Should he connive at any breach of the laws or of the settlement regulations, he will be considered as an accessary, and be liable to punishment accordingly.[3]

New arrivals soon discovered how rigorous was the life at Port Arthur, which from early morning operated like a smoothly run treadwheel. At the sound of the first bell, the men rose immediately, neatly folded their bedding and placed it in the middle of their berth. Fifteen minutes later, when the second bell rang, they removed their caps and jackets and washed 'in a proper manner'.[4] After a period of work they ate their monotonous but filling breakfast of bread and gruel (commonly called skilly), after which they washed and dried the eating utensils and ranged them on shelves, and the tables and benches were scrubbed. Then prayers were read, and work was resumed.

Any prisoner who refused to work was promptly punished. In 1848, nine chained men hauling three-wheeled carts, taking water or fuel to staff quarters, went on strike. They were told they had a choice: to continue to work or to go to the cells and be tried for insubordination. The men claimed that they could not work as they were not half as strong as they had been; slackness throughout the settlement had been tightened recently, and they no longer received extra food when they called at the officers' homes. The result of the strike was that eight of the men agreed to work and the only one who refused was sent to a cell. He was quickly released because 'in a minute he promised to be good'.[5]

Around the settlement and nearby there was constant activity. For example, in one day in 1846, splitters split wood; quarrymen quarried stone; washermen washed; a fisherman caught fish for the hospital patients; scavengers cleared drains; the water gang carried thousands of litres of water to the staff quarters, the military barracks and Point Puer; another gang kept the cows and cleaned the wheat; the garden gangs burned rubbish, cleared ground, cut hops, carted vegetables. There were 2 clerks in the superintendent's office and at the ship-building yard, 9 sub-constables, 1 groom, 8 gardeners, 28 servants, and 6 hospital wardsmen, and in a miscellaneous category of workers were cow and goat herds, schoolkeepers, lamplighters, gatekeepers, sextons, a barber and a flagellator.[6] In later years, prisoners would be employed at butchering, bullock-driving, milking, potting, salt-making, collecting seaweed and guano for manure, laying and repairing rail, tram, and macadamized roads, cutting grass for mats and brooms, and playing the church organ.[7]

In 1841, Linus Miller might be seen washing shirts. Although he thought he would prefer to go to the gallows than the wash-house, he was hardly in a position to refuse when he was offered this sought-after position. In *Notes of an Exile*, he wrote, with some sarcasm:

Every Monday morning 1300 shirts were divided among five men ... to be washed, dried, and returned to their respective owners. An over-seer presided over us to see that the work was properly done. For the first three weeks I rubbed the skin from my fingers, and found great difficulty in getting a tithe of the dirt off the shirts, which, when Saturday night came, presented a very sorry appearance. But the pleasantest part of my duty consisted in *serving out* the clean linen. The English prisoners were all enraged at the partiality shown me, and delighted at an opportunity of finding fault. 'Do you call that clean, you bloody long ——!' one would say, as he hove the really filthy shirt at my head; and a thousand insults were offered me, while I peddled them off. Some would even swear their shirts were dirtier than when I received them ...

In 1842, Henry Savery might be seen dying, in hospital, as in fact he was by David Burn, who was filled with horror and awe at 'the lack-lustre glare of his hollow eye'. Savery had been a prosperous sugar-refiner and a newspaper editor in Bristol, where he was convicted of forgery in 1825 and received the death sentence, which was commuted to transportation the day before the hanging was due.

Savery's first book, *The Hermit of Van Diemen's Land*, which was the first volume of Australian essays, was published in 1829, and had first appeared in the *Colonial Times*, although as a convict he was not permitted to write for the press. His wife followed him to the colony and was entrusted by her parents to the care of Algernon Montagu, who was said to have seduced her during the voyage. According to Burn, the story of the seduction, which circulated for many years, goaded Savery to frenzy. He related it in *Quintus Servinton*, the first, and now rare, Australian novel, which was published in three volumes in Hobart in 1830–1.

A view of a Port Arthur chain-gang showing how the centre chain extended from the ankles to the waist. The drawing is by the Quaker missionary, Frederick Mackie, who spent some time with the convicts there in 1851.

A late nineteenth-century view of the picturesque Exile Cottage, as it was then known. The Irish political prisoner, William Smith O'Brien, was confined in it.

Mrs Savery, who had 'made shipwreck of her husband's peace of mind', had returned to England in 1829. Savery attempted suicide, and Burn claimed that when he saw the miserable convict, the wound on his throat was 'scarce-healed'. Ironically, after Savery's second conviction for forgery, Judge Algernon Montagu had sentenced him to transportation to Port Arthur. Savery died on 6 February 1842, possibly from a stroke, and was buried in an unmarked grave, as were all convicts buried on the island. A plaque now commemorates his death and his contribution to Australian literature.[8]

At the picturesque cottage in which the Irish political prisoner, William Smith O'Brien, was confined in 1849 for about a year, he might be seen working in the garden. O'Brien had been tried for treason and sentenced to be hanged, drawn and quartered. The sentence was commuted to transportation for life, and in 1848 he arrived in the colony with five other Irish exiles. O'Brien refused to accept a ticket-of-leave and was sent to Darlington penal settlement at Maria Island, where he also lived alone in a cottage.

An oil painting of Port Arthur, in which men appear to be fishing or bathing. In the late 1830s prisoners were permitted to bathe in the bay, but after George Higgins drowned accidentally, a responsible person had to accompany them.

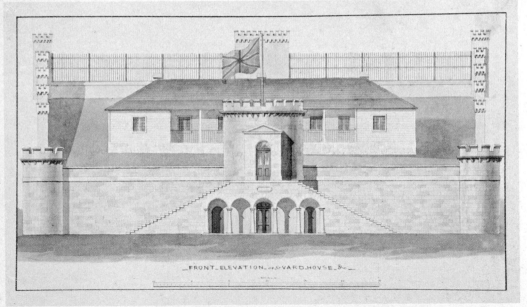

An undated miniature on ivory called 'First Man in Charge of Convicts, Port Arthur'.

An 1836 plan of the church. The foundation stone was laid on 25 April 1836.

A front elevation of the guard house and tower.

William Smith O'Brien.

After an escape attempt from the island, O'Brien was sent to Port Arthur, where, according to an officer of the Convict Department, John Evenden, he had the privilege of ordering his own provisions—even wine—through the commandant's office. Shortly before leaving the settlement, after he had accepted a ticket, O'Brien was granted permission to farewell the officers' children, and to each he gave a guinea and his wishes for future prosperity. Eventually, he returned to Europe where he was granted a free pardon in 1856, following the

The importance of food occupied so large a place in the minds of prisoners at Port Arthur that the Comptroller-General, W. Nairn, wrote in 1861 that it was one of the most significant aspects of their management:

the utmost attention should be paid to the food of the convicts. They are aware that the Government direct the food, however plain it may be, to be of the best quality; and they regard as a grievance any attempt to require them to consume food of inferior quality to that which they believe they are entitled to. At Port Arthur the utmost attention has always been paid to this point, and should any complaint arise ... the medical officer is the final authority....[10]

The poor quality of food in the 1830s had been caused largely by the difficulties of beginning a new settlement, and its isolation, although within ten years there was a considerable improvement. Fresh meat and vegetables had been introduced as soon as possible, but the menu continued to be monotonous. Eventually, the gruel was improved by the addition of rice and sugar or oatmeal and molasses, and the fresh beef or salt pork or salt beef was varied by the serving of fish. (In a table of equivalents used at the settlement, nearly 1 kilogram of fish was equal to nearly half a kilogram of fresh beef.) Even suet pudding was served in later years, but the Sunday treat of raisins for the Point Puer boys was denied the men at Port Arthur. A wide variety of vegetables was grown on the peninsula, although in 1848 cabbage must have been served all too frequently because 20 000 kilograms were produced.[11]

When the ban on smoking was lifted, a portion of bread was relinquished in return for tobacco. Colonel Godfrey Mundy inspected the mess-hall in 1851 and wrote facetiously in *Our Antipodes*: 'I was told that, if I waited until the meal was over, I should see a waiter going round with pipes and tobacco for such of the guests who desired a whiff of the Virginian weed.'

In the early 1840s, another visitor, David Burn, described the food as savoury and palatable, and he thought it 'not only ample but nutritious, consisting of excellent soup, good wheaten bread (I tasted both), and beef, mutton, or pork—such a meal, indeed, as would rejoice the heart and gladden the eyes of many an honest, hard-working, hungry Briton'.

Food was not ample, however, for men reported for idleness, because they received half rations in consequence, and the daily allowance of prisoners sentenced to solitary confinement was unlimited water and barely half a kilogram of bread daily. In solitary, the average loss of weight was a little over 3 kilograms in a week and nearly 11 in thirty days. 'Men of irritable and restless disposition lose most [weight], whilst obedient and quietly disposed men lose least.'[12]

On the whole, Port Arthur prisoners were well fed, although the scale of food received depended on, for example, behaviour, or whether the man was at hard or light labour. At light labour, prisoners received less food. Mundy thought the men appeared to be in stronger physical health than the soldiers stationed there: 'when I see a lot of burly fellows, not only muscular of limb and body, but absolutely *running to jowl*, common sense tells me that neither the mind nor the body are much overtaxed.' Although the treadwheel was no longer in use at the time of his visit, he wondered if it might be used to reduce some of the 'too solid flesh' on the ribs of peninsula prisoners.

Not surprisingly, leisure and entertainment were not features of a convict's life at Port Arthur. Perhaps only once a year, at Christmas, did the authorities relent and allow the day to be marked in a special way. An early reference to Christmas at Port Arthur, in Booth's journal in 1833, reveals that on the day before, he allowed prisoners to stop work early and to fish for the following day: the result was a cartload of shellfish and a huge haul of salmon. In the early 1840s, Christmas was even more festive, according to Martin Cash who was among prisoners, including those from the solitary cells, who assembled and were permitted to receive tea, sugar, tobacco or other gifts the staff chose to give them. A highlight of the day was a performance by another prisoner, the popular convict balladist, Francis McNamara, known as Frank the Poet, whose songs were sung by hundreds of convicts in Australia:

There was a stage erected in the centre of the yard, where comic and sentimental singing was to be heard. We had Portuguese Joe in the character of Darkey, and the famed Frank the Poet, who threw off a few extempore verses for the amusement of the company, at the same time giving his coat of arms, viz., 'My name is Frank McNamara, a native of Cashell, County Tipperary, sworn to be a tyrant's foe, and while I live I'll crow.'

McNamara had been tried at Kilkenny, Ireland, in 1832 and transported to Sydney, where in 1842 he was sentenced for being at large with firearms in his possession.

By 1860, the celebrations on Christmas Day reflected the more lenient attitude to prison discipline, roast beef and plum pudding being served to relieve the usual monotonous fare. The dinner and the concert following it were reported in detail by the *Mercury*:

At an establishment of this painful nature, where so much suffering and privation are necessarily felt, it was very pleasant to witness ... the little manifestation of joy in which the prisoners were permitted to indulge....

After divine service ... conducted with much solemnity, the prisoners assembled in the spacious dining hall, where few tables were to be seen without its roast beef and plum-pudding, and few mess tins without its quantam of tea. ... The repast, though limited, was amply sufficient to mark the distinction between Christmas and ordinary days, and was enjoyed less from its powers of satiety, than from its extreme novelty.

... the dining-hall ... became a scene of much mirth and festivity. Many comic songs, but more of a plaintive kind, were sung, while dancing and a few other pantomimic gyrations were kept up with much animation till nearly 5 o'clock. The greatest order and good nature prevailed amongst the prisoners, who, after supper . . . retired to the dormitory and cells, apparently much pleased with the frolics . . . and grateful no doubt. . . .

Another more regular relaxation, introduced as early as 1834, was an excellent library of general literature and religious and educational works of rich and varied contents. By 1834, several private individuals had donated a small collection of books and these useful and instructive works were read diligently in the scant spare time the men had, or while they were recovering from illness. The missionaries, Backhouse and Walker, reported to Arthur in 1834 that reading was 'at least, negatively beneficial', as a means of keeping the prisoners from 'evil' conversation, but the supply of books was inadequate.[13]

By the late 1850s, the number of books in the library had increased to about 2000, and the convict bookbinder was busily rebinding 716 volumes in 1863. By the late 1860s, the duties of the librarian, Joseph Hill, were far from onerous, because already the prisoners were few and the time spent on books 'almost infinitesmal'. By this time the men were allowed one book a week, but the rule was not rigidly enforced if a prisoner had 'a decided literary tendency', which must have been the exception rather than the rule. When the settlement closed in 1877, the library contained about 2000 books, even though many had been sent to the Cascades Invalid Depot and other penal institutions in Hobart.[14]

Many prisoners learnt reading, writing and elementary arithmetic at the settlement, although in 1848–9 nearly all the men had learnt to read before arriving in the colony. The convict, Linus Miller, described the school and the library while he was at Port Arthur in the early 1840s: 'School books were supplied by the government, and an excellent library of religious, historical, and miscellaneous works, provided by the liberality of private individuals who feel interested in the

A serene, late nineteenth-century view of a sentry-box in the foreground, a corner of the penitentiary, in front of which is a wall and drinking fountain, and the church. The spire was blown down during a storm in about 1875.

welfare of the prisoners. Many hundreds, who know not their A.B.C., here acquired a good common education'. Sometimes a literate man would give a lecture to his classmates. 'I heard one read a very capital lecture at the close of the school hour in the evening to some scores of his comrades, he as well as they being attired in a canary coloured suit', wrote Francis J. Cockburn in his *Letters from the Southern Hemisphere*. While some prisoners were at school, public reading was carried out in the dormitories at night, a practice introduced by Commandant James Boyd. One of the prisoners would read aloud from a book of general interest for the benefit of those who had defective eyesight or were not attending school that night.[15]

Church attendance could also be considered a relaxation. Until the church was built, the prisoners had gathered in the open air on fine Sunday mornings, under the watchful eye of the military, for a service performed 'in accents so clear and audible, so fervent, humble and devout'.[16] After the church was built, amid the clank of chains, the men marched to their wooden benches, and the convict choir to its place where it would chant the psalms, taught to them by a man especially appointed for the task, with 'considerable effect'.

All denominations worshipped together and for this reason the church was never consecrated. In 1843, however, an incident occurred that put a stop to non-Catholics and Catholics combining for services because about 185 Catholic prisoners took a bold stand and refused to attend services that were contrary to their creed. Booth respected their wishes, supplied them with Bibles and Testaments, and allowed them to gather in the schoolroom, with instructions to 'employ themselves in any devout manner they might think proper but to observe perfect quiet and order'. After this successful strike, the prisoners then refused to attend general prayers, and again Booth agreed to their request. These incidents resulted in the appointment of a Catholic chaplain to Port Arthur.[17]

In the late 1840s, major changes took place in staffing, management and discipline at the settlement. In the past, according to the regulations, the commandant's duties had been—or were supposed to be—strictly magisterial, but over the years had gradually included duties more properly those of the superintendent of convicts. In consequence, the responsibilities of the staff had been eroded. This was, according to the Lieut.-Governor, Sir William Denison, in 1848, 'a state of things I have no hesitation in saying, destructive of all effective discipline, and most injurious both to the men and the officers'. Because the discipline of the officers was lax and they lacked responsibility, they neglected their duty and were often involved in trafficking with the prisoners. The discipline of the prisoners had become both severe and relaxed and was 'altogether ineffective, either for punishment or reformation'.[18]

As Port Arthur had gradually increased in importance as a penal settlement, tradition frequently replaced written regulations, there was no chain of responsibility, and management had become difficult. Existing arrangements were almost impossible to improve, and the only solution was to sweep away the cumbrous and 'antiquated establishment' and to reorganize the whole. In 1848, it was decided to abolish the post of commandant and to appoint instead a superintendent of Port Arthur, although this arrangement operated only until 1853, when the title of civil commandant and superintendent was used.[19]

So, in 1848, there was a clean sweep of staff from the commandant down to convict overseers. William Thomas Napier Champ, who had replaced Booth in 1844, and was a firm, just and humane commandant for four years—'universally esteemed', according to Mortlock—left the settlement and retired to private life. He had clashed with Denison over criticism of the management at Port Arthur, which Champ mistakenly regarded as a reflection on him. Several years later, in 1852, he accepted Denison's offer of the important post of colonial secretary. He became the first premier of Tasmania, from 1856 to 1857, and from 1857 to 1868 he was the inspector-general of penal establishments in Victoria, where he was joined by some of the staff who had worked for him at the settlement.[20] At Port Arthur, Champ was replaced by George Courtenay.

In the early days of his appointment, Courtenay busied himself by writing to his superiors about the deficiencies of the settlement: 'every day brought something new to light'. He explained how no one, from the lowest convict upwards, was accustomed to receiving orders from anyone but the commandant. 'I have heard one convict say quite seriously to another, "If anyone insults me I shall go to the Commandant"; he had no idea that the smallest power to redress his wrong could be vested in any one else'.[21]

The staff had become 'the most useless set of beings on the face of the earth'. They were so used to receiving orders from the commandant that if they disliked an order they set to work to argue the point. Meanwhile, the reasons given for peculiarities were that 'it has been the case here for a long time' or 'it has always been so'. Not the least of the oddities was that convict servants had been allowed to wander in the bush in search of firewood or ferns, but though they had a pass from their master, neither the superintendent of convicts nor anyone else knew where they were. Men had been allowed out on loan to staff for sixpence a day for the most unlikely purposes—one to play jugglers' tricks and another, a man of particularly bad character, to play the fiddle for an officer. This state of affairs was ill suited to a penal settlement and could not and would not be allowed to continue.

Not only was the staff reorganized. The old regulations were replaced largely by those operating at probation stations, and the chief difference between them and Port Arthur was to be that the settlement received reconvicted prisoners and other troublesome men. Even the settlement's title was changed, as the *Hobart Town Courier* reported in August 1848: 'The penal settlement of Port Arthur no longer exists. By public sign-boards it is notified that it is only a "house of correction". The staff of officers has been very much reduced.' Despite this announcement, Port Arthur continued to be known as a penal settlement.

William Thomas Napier Champ, the commandant of Port Arthur from 1844 to 1848. He became the first premier of Tasmania.

6 Our Town

For the staff and their families, life at Port Arthur was similar to life in any other town, although it lacked shops, hotels and certain amenities. Because it was a penal settlement, regulations were to be developed that must at times have been restrictive, particularly one that prevented its residents from leaving the settlement whenever they wished. To leave, everyone required the commandant's permission, and staff members were allowed leave of absence, to Hobart only, not more than once in six months unless in urgent circumstances.[1] Despite its disadvantages, however, Port Arthur became the home of hundreds of families during its history—families with children who were born there and christened there, and sometimes died there, at a tender age, and were buried on the Isle of the Dead. Port Arthur was 'our town' to its free residents.

To David Burn, who visited the settlement in the early 1840s, Port Arthur was 'a place of wonders' where 'the seeds of religion and virtue have been carefully planted'. Twice on Sundays, worshippers strolled along a leafy avenue to seat themselves on cushioned pews, while the prisoners marched to their wooden benches and the convict choir took its place. The children of the settlement attended Sunday school and Burn wrote a description of its anniversary celebration, which also reveals something of the social life of Port Arthur:

A number of excellent instructive books were provided as prizes for

A mid 1840s view of Port Arthur, with Mount Arthur in the background. The ship may be the Lady Franklin, *which was built in the dockyard at Port Arthur. The large semaphore can be clearly seen on the hill at left.*

the most exemplary attendents, the most diligent and proficient scholars. In each branch a hot competition ensued; and in many instances, so earnest was the struggle, that Captain Booth, the patron of the institution, felt some difficulty in awarding the palm. The examination over, the children proceeded to a marquee, formed of the *Favourite*'s sails and flags, and tastefully adorned with a profusion of native wreaths and gardens. In this marquee they enjoyed a fête *al fresco*; tea, coffee, cake, raspberries, gooseberries, currants, and other fruits, being bountifully supplied. It was an era in *their* lives—an event of pleasant contemplation to the spectators. The children satisfied, a like refreshment was next provided for their delighted parents....

Despite the influence of religion at Port Arthur, parents were wary of exposing their children, not to mention themselves, to what some of them considered was an unhealthy moral influence. Yet the parents were not immune to the influence. According to the Reverend Robert Crooke, a chaplain on the peninsula, although certain subjects were generally avoided even among men, they were openly discussed among mothers of families who would 'unreservedly speak of unnatural crime' (as sodomy was often called at the time).[2] The families of staff attempted to avoid the prisoners—unless they had well-behaved men working for them—and the medical officer, Dr Thomas Brownell, who was very aware of his responsibilities as a parent, thought their influence so harmful that in the early 1840s he wished he and his family were anywhere but Port Arthur. The families frequently witnessed crime and punishment, he wrote, and 'the mind becomes inured and the fine feelings blunted, so that what at first appears shocking and revolting is apt to soften down to a lighter grade and sin is not seen and felt to be so exceedingly sinful as it should be'.[3]

Brownell's doubts about his family's situation must have been strengthened in 1843 when he was stabbed in the neck by a murderer, William Langham, who had a knife concealed in his sleeve when the doctor called to attend to him. Even after this unnerving experience, Brownell remained dedicated to what he described as a 'first class appointment', and lived at Port Arthur until the late 1850s. In 1850, his comment that the settlement had been, in the early 1840s, 'truly awful' and 'in or out of the Bottomless Pit, greater depravity could not have been collected together', suggests that an improvement had taken place.

Many families were in daily contact with convict servants and tutors or a few assigned female servants who were the only women convicts permitted at the settlement. David Burn's daughter, Jermima Frances, lived at Port Arthur with her husband in the early 1840s, and decades later she recalled her experience of convict servants: 'We used to have [convicts] as servants and some of them had worked in the best houses in England. You can have no idea what good work they used to do and how much we came to like some of them.'[4]

Prisoners could be employed privately and legitimately, but at times the system was abused. In the late 1840s, for example, prisoners took parties shooting or fishing, and were sent on messages all over the peninsula and no one knew where they were to be found. So slack was the discipline at this time that one prisoner was given a pass to stay out late in order to play juggler's tricks at the Lemprieres' home; another was ordered to play the fiddle for an officer.[5]

Some families, depending on their social standing, preferred to employ a governess or a convict tutor (an educated man), rather than send their children to the government school at Port Arthur, where spelling, reading, writing, geography, arithmetic and needlework were taught. In 1837, the Lemprieres' governess was far from satisfactory. 'Miss Wood in a tremendous mood ... because I could not let her have any spirits', wrote Thomas Lempriere in his diary. 'Drank herself drunk today with honey beer—disgraceful—she shall not stop here.'

Miss Wood soon left and in the early 1840s the young Canadian prisoner, Linus Miller, lived with the family for more than two years as tutor to their eleven children. After working in a timber-carrying gang and at lighter labour—in the garden, the wash-house and as clerk of the church—he was delighted to find 'such a *home*, and *friends*, in *such* a *land*', as he wrote in *Notes of an Exile*. Thomas Lempriere was equally impressed with Miller, describing him as a man with 'honourable feelings'.

Another prisoner, John Mortlock, was employed as a tutor in about 1850 by a chaplain, the Reverend Edward Durham. In his *Experiences of a Convict*, Mortlock wrote that he became 'much attached' to his 'lively, roguish pupils and their good-looking mamma'. The clergyman, Crooke, described Mortlock as a gentleman in 'appearance, manner and conversation' who 'never associated or conversed with his fellow prisoners who all had a sort of respect for him'.

The serious nature of the settlement did not prevent staff and their families from taking every opportunity to enjoy their life at Port Arthur:

When everything was in first-rate order, and 'bolters' were not abroad, every man, woman, and child who could be spared from duty, and who belonged to the 'society' of the place, or had a claim upon its countenance, used to turn out for open-air enjoyment. Such horse-racing on the sandy beaches, such picnicking in the shady groves, such balls, parties, and general merriment, existed nowhere else, and rendered the settlement a not altogether unpleasant place of exile. It mattered little that the prisoners were groaning under their chains, or fainting under the lash; for men grow hardened by frequent contact with suffering....[6]

Booth's journal reveals him as a sociable man, looking forward to cosy evenings with friends and to dinners and balls, and as 'father of the Bachelors' he entertained fellow officers on Christmas Day, when 'the thoughts of Home would come to mind and cause a gloom'. He eyed the girls in Hobart with interest, and at Sorell, near Tasman Peninsula, he commented on 'a fine buxom young lass' who turned out to be the daughter of one of his charges.

Booth was fond of the Lempriere family and frequently visited their home, spinning yarns until a late hour, playing his guitar 'in a superior manner' according to Lempriere, who drew his portrait, or perhaps discussing the first issue of the Port Arthur Gazette, compiled by Lempriere on 12 April 1834. A christening was a special occasion in 1833, when Booth donned full dress uniform to be godfather to Charlotte Lempriere, after which there was a party he described as 'on a very respectable scale for a Penal Settlement'. In the following year, he became godfather to his servant's child and to the Reverend John Manton's, and recorded 'another bouncing girl' born to the Lemprieres.

To help fill the leisure hours in the 1830s there was 'capital sport' in the bay with a whale 'until it got away, spouting blood', kangarooing with guns and dogs, fishing, and hunting for 'badgers' (wombats) that might be cooked like sucking pig. Nor was boat-racing neglected. In 1834, Booth and Lempriere organized a race of four of the commandant's crew against the crack whaleboat manned by six amateurs, after which the ladies joined in for a picnic at Point Puer. There were always homely pleasures, too, such as gardening: Booth grew strawberries 'in perfection' and was annoyed when a hot wind 'played Old Harry' with his gooseberries.

From time to time the local entertainment was augmented when a ship such as the French frigate *L'Artemise* anchored in the bay. On the morning of her arrival, in February 1839,

The Port Arthur brass band.

Captain La Place welcomed officers and their families to 'an elegant Tiffin and a set of quadrilles' on board the ship, and Booth returned the compliment by straining the resources of the settlement to make the occasion agreeable.[7] A ride on the convict-propelled railway proved popular, and the ship's officers were ecstatic during a steep descent: 'down they went, hollowing, shouting, screaming like madmen'.[8]

Eventually the settlement grew to include a literary institute, regattas of six-oared boats, a brass band, and a cricket club which played on 'a very good wicket' on the esplanade—married cricketers playing 'singles' or non-smokers playing smokers—and if a ship sailed into the bay the club's secretary soon tried to arrange a match with the officers.[9] The institute was commonly called the officers' library and reading room, and in the opinion of an anonymous writer of the 1860s, it was 'the fashionable resort of Port Arthur dunces'.[10] Well stocked with the latest literature, by the 1870s it was a library in little more than name, and the staff were by then jointly subscribing to two Hobart journals, and the *Australasian, Home News, Illustrated London News* and *Punch.*

The institute was also used for socials and other entertainment: On Her Majesty's birthday we let off our pent up feelings by tripping it on the light fantastic toe until the small hours of the morning—but . . . some of the poor officers, and constables, did not seem to enter fully into the spirit of the thing until the Commandant had retired, and the rum punch had been brewed and imbibed, ah it was a great sight to see how the poor creatures' spirits rose. . . .[11]

The commandant who hindered the festivities, James Boyd, was a fine-looking Scotsman who was the civil commandant and superintendent from 1853 to 1871, after having gained experience at Pentonville Prison in England, Maria Island penal settlement, and the Hobart penitentiary. Not surprisingly, he was heartily disliked by some of the prisoners, but to many, especially the well behaved, he was said to be very kind, considerate, and even indulgent.

To the staff he could be 'autocratical and over-bearing', particularly if they 'had the temerity to differ from him'.[12] Nevertheless, in 1866, the staff honoured the Boyds—Mrs Boyd for her 'amiable qualities' and Mr Boyd for his interest in the social and intellectual advancement of the staff. A deputation presented Boyd's portrait to his wife, and a similar portrait—'a true likeness executed in oil colours' by the artist and photographer Alfred Bock—was unveiled in the library. A few days later Boyd received an address 'elegantly engrossed in vellum in illuminated characters by a resident'.[13]

Although no hotel existed at Port Arthur until after it closed, in 1853 a charming cottage—known as Government Cottage—was built for official visitors, such as the lieut.-governor. It was a single-storeyed building next to the church. From the verandah, which was covered with roses and creepers, there was a sweeping view of the splendidly landscaped public garden and also the bay. Since the late 1830s, oaks, elms and ash trees presented by the Lieut.-Governor, Sir John Franklin, had been thriving in this area. But the garden, which was so admired by visitors and enjoyed by the residents, was established in the mid 1840s by William Champ, soon after he became the commandant. When Champ had been offered the position, he nearly declined after visiting the settlement for the first time, and wrote to his father that he was by no means pleased with the prospect of going there.

Champ did replace Booth and moved to the settlement with his wife, Helen Abigail, and their children. Whether it was at his wife's urging, or his own idea, he soon improved the settlement's appearance with the landscaping of a very pretty public garden, which he believed was most wanted for the ladies of the settlement to walk in. He was determined to collect a variety of plants for it. They included camellias and carnations grown from seed sent by his mother, whom he also asked 'to gather, while walking in the woods, seeds of wildflowers, also crabapple and blackberries'.[14]

In 1847, in the *Van Diemen's Land Royal Kalendar and Almanack,* a writer described the scene in the public garden:

In the centre of the main walk a fountain, with a jet of several feet, throws up continually a shower of water, which, after falling from a

Amateur Theatrical Performance, Port Arthur.

30th October 1865.

This Evening will be performed the laughable and amusing Farce of

"The Silent Woman."

— Dramatis Personae. —

Marianne Sandford, — Mrs Pilcher.   Mr Sandford, ___ Mr F. Maguinness.

Arthur Merton, ___ Mr Hill.

To be followed by Negro Minstrelsy.

— Songs. —

The Avon Hunt. _____ Wait for the Waggon.
Lily Dale. _____ Stop dat knockin'.

After which   An Irish Jig   will be danced by Mr Sweeney.

The whole to conclude

with   The 'Tigant' Farce   called

— "THE IRISH TUTOR." —

— Dramatis Personae. —

Mr Tilwell. _____ Mr F. Maguinness.   Dr O'Toole. ⎫
Charles, his Son. ___ ... Aherne.   Teddy O'Rourke. ⎬ ___ Mr Hill.
Dr Flail. _____ ... Keith.   Rosa, Tilwell's Niece. ___ Mrs Pilcher.
The Beadle. _____ ... S. Smith.   Mary, her Maid. Miss F. Maguinness.

Villagers, Attendants, &c.

Doors open at 7.30 P.M., — Performance to commence at 8 P.M. precisely.

— VIVAT REGINA. —

Stage Manager, Mr Lawson.   Acting Manager, Mr Hill.

A programme dated 1865 of an amateur theatrical performance at Port Arthur.
(Letitia Pilcher was appointed schoolmistress in 1863 and Joseph Hill became
the librarian in 1864.)

James Boyd, who was commandant of Port Arthur from 1853 to 1871, with his
hack, Peter, photographed near the guard tower. Alfred Bock took the
photograph.

A cricket team at Port Arthur, photographed by Alfred Bock sometime between
1855 and 1865.

The public garden established by William Champ in the mid 1840s, showing the fountain at left, which can be seen today, and the church and Government Cottage, in about 1860. The verandah of the cottage had a canvas awning.

pyramidical series of shelves into a basin, is carried underground to a canal, which besides its refreshing appearance affords the water necessary for irrigating the plants. Rustic benches are placed in the different walks. There is also a summerhouse at the highest part of the ground . . . this place is a favourite resort for the officers and their families.

Not many years later, the canal resembled 'a sweet little stream' and a weeping willow had spread its branches over the summer-house. In this haven it was easy for a visitor, Henry Butler Stoney, to forget that so many prisoners were in chains nearby.[15] At Port Arthur and in the colony generally, prisoners in chains were a common sound and sight, and one few people could easily forget. In Hobart, Launceston, Oatlands and other towns, men in chain-gangs were undergoing colonial sentences, and gangs of up to 200 men were passing almost continually along the capital's most fashionable streets. At the first sight of the chain-gangs, a feeling of horror crept over the visitor: 'nor does he overcome the sensation, until his ear

In the 1840s, some attractive homes were built at Port Arthur. From left, the houses are the assistant surgeon's (built 1848), the Catholic chaplain's (1843), the medical officer's (about 1847), the commissariat officer's (about 1845) and the Church of England chaplain's (1842). The latter was badly damaged during a fire in the late nineteenth century and is now single-storeyed. In the foreground is the prisoners' first penitentiary. By this time, in about 1854, the English trees in the church avenue were well established and the stone columns at the entrance can be seen.

becomes habituated to the music of chains, as they are rung by the convicts at their work'.[16]

In the 1850s, at Port Arthur, a visiting Quaker missionary, Frederick Mackie, found 'the clanking of chains was dreadful, being heavy the noise is so great that it is heard a considerable distance'.[17] In contrast, another visitor was struck with 'the silence and indescribable air of seriousness' of the settlement.[18] Silence was an unlikely word to apply to the settlement in view of the chain-gangs, but serious it certainly was. And for the free, probably more in an attempt to come to terms with their environment than from callousness, they led lives that were as normal as could be in the circumstances.

A 1981 view of the three houses at left in the previous picture.

Another 1981 view, showing the houses close to the church on the corner of Champ and Church streets.

Eventually, visitors not only spent holidays at Port Arthur with friends who lived there, but were attracted to the wildness and beauty of Eaglehawk Neck, which was in fact a prison doorway, where the main objects of its residents were to prevent the escape of prisoners and to check the official passes of anyone who wished to cross it. In 1835, a young lieutenant, 23-year-old Henry Bunbury, who was in command at Eaglehawk Neck, thought it was a very odd place with a very odd name. Nevertheless, he was supremely content in his little wooden house, and wrote in a letter a rare, early description of Eaglehawk Neck at that time:

I have a sergeant ... and 25 men under me, besides a chain of 11 watch dogs, which, with two sentries, watch the isthmus.... The only things I have to do are to write my name on the back of letters leaving the Peninsula, and not to leave home when any prisoner has absconded; just what any sensible man would wish as he might chance to be murdered if he met the ruffian in the bush.

I live in a rickety little wooden house at the foot of a gloomy, thickly-wooded hill, within 200 yards of the sea, which nearly always breaks with a heavy surf on the fine sandy beach of Pirates' Bay. I have a whaleboat and convict crew at my command, so that I can go anywhere I like ... but my chief amusement is my garden.... I am vulgar enough to grow potatoes and cabbage and onions, but I think the salt rations are a sufficient excuse. Nothing else whatever is to be had for love or money, unless I am successful kangaroo hunting.... I never feel dull or lonely, but find the days too short for all my various employments, and in the evening my books pass the time pleasantly.[19]

In the 1850s, when visitors were enjoying frequent excursions to the area, the Lieut.-Governor, Sir William Denison, chose to spend a family holiday at Eaglehawk Neck. 'My Dearest Mother', he wrote in a letter quoted in *Varieties of Viceregal Life*, 'here we are, C[aroline] and self and nine children and three servants, squeezed up into a little cottage on the sea shore of Pirates' Bay. This would not appear to offer much comfort, but the barracks are close at hand, in which resides a soldier and his wife, who act as cook, housemaid, and general factotums. My manservant sleeps there, and I have a boat's crew of convicts who cut wood for us, fetch water, and take us out fishing.'

Lady Denison soon began to like being there rather better than she had at first, despite the primitive conditions, having to bring furniture and provisions from Government House, and a near encounter with an escaped prisoner. While walking along the beach with the children, she met a soldier, who said, ' "It is not very safe for you to be along the shore here to-day, because there is a *bolter out!!*" ' Although this was apparently an unfamiliar term to Lady Denison, she soon guessed the meaning, but as they were all anxious for more information, they followed the man. He was 'loitering slowly along, and peeping up into every little ravine' near the shore.

Lady Denison asked the soldier if there was an escaped convict about, to which he replied that it was pretty certain, from the time that had passed since his escape, that the man would reach the Neck that night, if he was not captured beforehand.

'And are you sent here to watch for him?' I asked. 'No, Ma'am,' said the man, with a *naivete* that rather amused me, 'I am only looking out for my interest, you see, because we get a reward of two pounds if we apprehend him, but they are so desperate sometimes, that it takes two or three men to master them, unless one was to kill him on the spot, which of course one would not *quite like* to do!' I did not exactly see, after all, what danger the children or I had to apprehend from a man whose interest it would so evidently be to avoid our observation; however . . . I . . . hastened home with the children. . . .

The next morning, Lady Denison was relieved to learn that the poor wretched prisoner had been captured, although the soldier on the beach had not been fortunate enough to catch him.[20]

Anyone who wished to cross Eaglehawk Neck and arrived without a pass issued by the colonial secretary had a choice of returning by the same route or waiting for a signal to be sent to the commandant at Port Arthur. Because the regulation regarding official passes was so well known, few people would have arrived without one. Even so, in the 1860s, a group reached the Neck without their 'passports'. One of the party recorded the experience in a tourist publication, *Guide for Excursionists from the Mainland to Tasmania*:

We must go back. Go back! a nice thing indeed; forty miles of back country got over since sunrise, and forty more to retrace. No such thing! Well, we can telegraph . . . for leave to enter; or, if the worst comes to the worst, as we look like gentlemen, we may be allowed to sleep on the benches. We prefer to telegraph, and we go into the guard-house, and are requested civilly to sit down.

While waiting, the visitors offered a cigar to the guard, 'a fine veteran of a fellow', who was cleaning his gun, and two other guards were 'lounging outside, apparently in doubt whether they are awake or asleep'. By this time, the soldiers at Eaglehawk Neck had been withdrawn, having been replaced in 1859 by a police guard, although a detachment of troops remained at Port Arthur until 1863.[21] The veteran was disgruntled: 'A man been't a hanimal; a man has his feelings, and can't be merely fed up like a pig. He wants his chums, and here there is nothing but them everlasting dogs, and waves as keeps roaring away for ever.'

At last a message arrived from the commandant and the travellers were able to 'freely enter into the enchanted ground of all wickedness'. As they made their way along the road, they turned back to see 'under the rosy light of the declining sun the two sentinels verging once more into a quiet doze, and the veteran of the pipe looking steadfastly after us, and then turning to gaze upon the roaring surf'.

7 Punishments

One view of Port Arthur, in 1836, was that 'misery of the deepest dye' existed there and the sufferings of the wretched prisoners were the consequences of their own wickedness.[1] But in 1853, the Quaker missionary, Frederick Mackie, wrote that the brutality suffered at the settlement was largely caused by an evil system. To him, it was 'a heart-sickening and dreadful sight' that man should become 'so brutalized that he must be treated like a wild beast', but he believed it was not entirely the fault of the prisoners. Conditions had improved, although it would be a long time before 'the evil engendered will be rooted out' at Port Arthur.[2]

The most startling changes at the settlement had already occurred before Mackie first visited it, and concerned the types of punishments there. During the 1840s, coinciding with more 'enlightened' methods of penal discipline in Britain, several of the cruellest and most humiliating punishments had ceased. By the late 1840s, stonebreaking while chained in a stall similar to a dog kennel, dragging a log of wood chained to leg-irons, and flogging were no longer punishments, while soon the treadmill, so admired by the authorities when it was introduced in 1845, would also be discontinued. But the wearing of leg-irons by some prisoners remained a punishment until the settlement was abandoned in 1877, fewer men wearing them as the years passed.

Although certain punishments ceased, discipline remained unrelaxed at Port Arthur. Misconduct and minor infringements of the regulations were punished remorselessly and appear again and again on the prisoners' conduct records. For defacing a book, for example, William Dawson received fourteen days' solitary confinement and for disfiguring a prisoner by cutting off his hair, seven days' solitary. William May was sentenced to terms in leg-irons, in the chain-gang or to solitary confinement for 'making away with' his government clothing or wilfully destroying it, on eight separate occasions, and for having a turnip in his possession. James Martin, whose record fills pages, spent ten days in solitary for refusing to work on the treadwheel.

On four occasions, John Richard was sentenced to solitary confinement for 'positively refusing to attend the place of Divine Worship on the Sabbath'. Henry Brown's punishment for having a quantity of gooseberry wine was three months' hard labour. Another prisoner, John Bannon, spent ten days in solitary confinement for altering his clothes. It was the custom for men to go into partnership, each save an old pair of 'magpie' trousers when new clothing was issued, and give them to a convict tailor at the settlement who would separate the two pairs. By joining black to black and yellow to yellow, he would make one pair of black trousers and one of yellow. The prisoner's number was removed from the latter with soft soap and turpentine and they were dyed. The trousers were sold to

---

Originally a stonemason, James Martin was court-martialled in Barbados in 1842 for 'a breach of the articles of war'. His many punishments at Port Arthur, to which he was sentenced several times, included twelve months' hard labour in chains in 1855. His other sentences to the settlement were for absconding, housebreaking and larceny.

soldiers at the settlement. Bannon's clothing may have been altered like this.[3]

Sometimes the punishments a prisoner received could extend his sentence of transportation. In 1847, during an inspection of Port Arthur, Sir William Denison was approached by a man who had been sent to the settlement for a year and had been there for four due to misconduct. In *Varieties of Vice-regal Life*, Sir William wrote compassionately:

The poor fellow spoke to me with tears in his eyes, and ... I decided to try whether I could not, by speaking to him, persuade him to attempt to keep himself out of the fangs of the law for a short time. I saw him the next morning, and spoke to him seriously, yet kindly; and the poor fellow said that nobody, since he had been in the colony, had ever spoken to him in that manner before. I told him that if he would conduct himself well for three months, I would release him; and I spoke to the officers at the station to give him a chance—not to be too hard upon him.

This case moved both Sir William and his wife, who wrote to a friend: 'Did I tell you ... about the poor convict who touched W's feelings so much at Port Arthur?' She went on to say that her husband had since received a good report on the man's behaviour and 'had the pleasure of signing his pass', which released him from Port Arthur. Sir William believed that if more reliance could be placed on the staff, it would be possible for individual cases to be treated on their merits, thus avoiding such situations.

Meanwhile, sometime in the mid 1840s, the stonebreaking stalls on the waterfront near the commandant's house ceased to be used, although stonebreaking lingered as a punishment and was later carried out in a large shed built for the purpose. In 1847, John Sweatman, an officer on H.M.S. *Bramble*, which called at Port Arthur during a surveying expedition, noticed that the treadwheel had replaced the stalls. 'The "buck stalls" ... in which certain hopelessly incorrigible ruffians were chained

to break stones were now removed', he wrote, 'and a large treadmill erected instead on which I saw 60 men at once working in chains, grinding Corn for the Commissariat.'[4] The stalls were side by side and in each a man was chained to a ring set in the wall. All day he stood in front of a bench and broke stones, probably for roadmaking, with a hammer.

A clergyman on the peninsula, the Reverend Robert Crooke, also described these stalls:

Soldiers with loaded firelocks, and fixed bayonets, walk in front of these men, who are unchained and taken to their meals under a strong military guard, and when their day's labour is concluded marched under an escort to their sleeping places. These are men who are considered too dangerous to be allowed any liberty whatever, and are looked upon as being little better than wild beasts, and indeed the treatment they receive seems quite enough to destroy any small remains of humanity they may ever have possessed.[5]

This punishment was well known to William Derrincourt, who endured it himself, and to John Frost, but both described how the men were locked to a long chain. Apparently the stalls were built sometime in the early 1840s to separate the prisoners, preventing the wretched men from burying the hammers in each other's skulls.

One of the most peculiar sights at Port Arthur was to see men wearing leg-irons to which a log of wood was attached and which dragged along the ground, adding to the weight of the irons, wherever the prisoner went. After Derrincourt was removed from stonebreaking, he was given lighter irons and the log as well—a punishment reserved for habitual absconders and other men of bad character.[6]

In *Old Convict Days*, Derrincourt described 'the log': 'In this harness I was set to work at several jobs ... and besides carrying my loads as before, had to drag the log after me, not daring to lift it or to put a hand to it in any way. At night I ... put it under my head for a pillow.' Martin Cash dreaded 'the log', more because it deprived him of every chance of escape than for its weight and inconvenience. Both he and Linus Miller described how the log was carried while the prisoners were working, a more likely explanation than one describing how it was carried for a distance, while the men rested and then returned to the place of starting.

To many prisoners the treadwheel may have been the most painful punishment apart from flogging, which ceased in Tasmania in 1848. When the treadwheel at Port Arthur operated for the first time, in 1845, Commandant Champ confidently predicted that it would be an excellent punishment to discourage potential offenders, but by 1851 it was no longer in use. By this time there were only 600 or so men at the settlement and apparently too few men were sentenced to it, so the wheel could not operate.[7]

Strong, active prisoners were said to become accustomed to enduring the treadwheel, while others experienced dreadful suffering and pain. At Coldbath Fields Prison in England, feigned sickness and self-inflicted wounds were common ways of avoiding this punishment. After fifteen minutes on the wheel, one team of prisoners—exhausted, flushed and perspiring—came down from the steps to rest, while another team replaced it. The steps on the wheel resembled floats on a paddlewheel:

they move their legs as if they were mounting a flight of stairs; but with this difference, that instead of their *ascending*, the steps pass from under them, and . . . it is this peculiarity which causes the labour to be so tiring, owing to the want of a firm tread.[8]

The treadwheel at Port Arthur, like the ones at Coldbath Fields and Pentonville Prisons, may have been divided into narrow compartments, each with a hand-rail for the prisoner to grasp, and separated by wooden partitions. On the other hand, if it was similar to the smaller one in Hobart, it would not have had

A view of two prisoners on the treadwheel, probably at Hobart.

compartments. According to Linus Miller's description of the latter, 'every four minutes one of the men descended from the wheel at one end, while another mounted it at the other; each man upon the wheel periodically shifting two feet towards the place of descent'.

Throughout the settlement's history, there were always a number of prisoners wearing leg-irons, but the heaviest irons were gradually phased out after the late 1850s, when comparatively few men wore even light ones. As late as the early 1870s, however, prisoners who had received severe sentences were

Prisoners working the treadwheel at Coldbath Fields Prison in England.

placed, on arrival, in light irons for temporary safety and to allow time to improve their conduct. In 1853, when the population was about 700, a hundred men wore heavy leg-irons; in 1871, none wore heavy irons and only five were temporarily in light ones.[9]

Leg-irons varied in weight from about 6 kilograms to 18 kilograms, and possibly some of the heaviest weighed as much as 27. Daily, the prisoners wearing them turned up their trouser legs and were examined to see that the irons were firmly in place. The men were responsible for keeping the irons in good condition, but they frequently managed to 'oval' the irons, perhaps with a heavy stone, so that they could slip their ankles out.[10] John Perrott was punished on four occasions for having his irons split, broken, ovalled or loose, and many other men were punished for similar reasons.

After Martin Cash's first attempt to escape from Port Arthur, he was fitted with irons. He had swum across the bay at Eaglehawk Neck, but was soon captured on Forestier Peninsula and returned to the settlement, where he was sentenced to eighteen months in a chain-gang. The exploit impressed the other prisoners, as well as the blacksmith who fitted the leg-irons. 'I was fitted with a very light pair', Cash wrote, 'the blacksmith appearing to give himself a great deal of trouble in the selection. There are several sorts of irons, some of which are

William Forster, who was transported at the age of seventeen in 1843 for stealing a writing desk. (Unlike some convicts, he could read and write . . .) He was a farm labourer originally and was stout with a ruddy complexion, dark brown hair and black eyes. Sometime after 1855, he was sentenced to be hanged but was instead sent to Port Arthur. There he was punished for absconding, assault, disobeying orders, and misconduct, and spent two terms in the separate prison.

altered by the blacksmith, who frequently gets [a] tip for a pair of light ones, as it is a matter of no little consequence to the wearer, and as I had nothing to offer I expected something in a very different style, but I was most agreeably deceived. I mention this in order to show the feeling . . . towards me by my own class simply because I had crossed the Neck.'

After leg-irons were removed, the prisoner had difficulty in keeping his balance. As a visitor to Port Arthur observed: 'He would seem to be decidedly topheavy. He would lift his feet very high off the ground, and stagger about very much after the fashion of a man that had taken too much strong drink.'[11]

Despite Booth's distaste for flagellation, a startling number of lashes was distributed on the various stations on Tasman Peninsula while he was the commandant. In 1841, for example, 684 convicts received 18 469 lashes, including 6493 at the Point Puer boys' settlement.[12] But after Pentonville Prison was built in England in 1842 as a model prison that featured silence and the separation of prisoners, flogging was less favoured generally, slowly decreased, and was abandoned in Tasmania in 1848. At Port Arthur in 1847–8, in eight months, only five extremely bad characters were flogged, receiving a total of 108 lashes.

Many prisoners became defiant and hardened after flagellation, and John Frost gave as an example a very decent, well-behaved young man who was reported by 'an old drunken vagabond of an overseer' for having his hands in his pockets:

That young man was put into the cells; three days afterwards he was tried by the commandant [Booth] and sentenced to receive thirty-six lashes. I saw him flogged; and what effect had that punishment upon him? It made him one of the worst men on the station. He became an entirely different man, and . . . was continually receiving punishment, occasioned solely by the degrading manner in which he had been treated.

According to Frost, the convict flagellator at this time 'felt a gratification in inflicting and witnessing human misery. There were many prisoners who would bear any punishment rather than complain; I am certain that they would have died at the triangle rather than utter a groan'.

In despair, defiance and revenge, prisoners would sometimes set fire to the wooden triangles to which they had been strapped for a flogging. William Derrincourt was one of them.

After he was transferred to the coal mines near Port Arthur, he was lashed for misconduct. 'The first few falls of the cat [-o'-nine-tails] were enough to take my breath away and to draw blood freely, although comparatively lightly laid on.' Defiantly, he sang as loudly as he could a well-known and appropriate song:

> If I had a donkey what wouldn't go,
> Do you think I'd wallop him? Oh, dear, no.

When the opportunity arose, Derrincourt and another man placed the triangles on a wheelbarrow, took them to a kiln, and burned 'the horrid machine'.

In 1853, James Boyd became the commandant of Port Arthur. He had been employed at Pentonville Prison before his arrival in the colony, was trained in the management and discipline of the separate prison, and enthusiastic about its benefits. A year before his appointment to the settlement, the separate prison, modelled on Pentonville, was completed. When Boyd left Port Arthur in 1871, he was proud that he had never used flogging during his twenty-two years' service in the Convict Department of the colony. 'This striking fact has led to the abolition of flogging as a prison punishment', he announced confidently to his superiors, but inaccurately, since flagellation had been abolished by the authorities in 1848.[13] The greatest changes in punishment and discipline took place during his command, coinciding with new approaches to penal discipline. But he was an enlightened commandant, even if he was fond of congratulating himself on his success in reports to his superiors.

Executions were common in the early years of the colony and mass hangings occasionally occurred. The first was in April 1821, when ten men, whose crimes ranged from stealing animals to robbery with violence were hanged, but not one was a murderer. During Lieut.-Governor Arthur's term of office from 1824 to 1836, 260 executions took place, and in 1826, over five days, twenty-three men, escorted by javelin men (convict police) went to the gallows.[14] Slowly, the decrease of public executions occurred, and the opinion grew that hanging should be the penalty for murder alone. In the 1860s, executions had become rare events in the colony, but only a decade or so earlier, in 1852, a suggested coat of arms for Tasmania had been defined in rhyming heraldics:

> Two posts standant,
> One beam crossant,
> One rope pendant,
> One knave on the end on't.[15]

A number of prisoners committed vicious murders at the settlement and were tried at the Supreme Court in Hobart. Some, but not all, sank to such desperation that they chased the gallows, committing 'the most barbarous murders, in open sight of their companions and superiors with no other professed intention' than to be sent to court to receive the death sentence.[16] But usually the murders were ascribed to some cause, such as the tyranny of convict overseers, as in the case of Francis Maxfield, who was forced to carry a heavy load by Joseph Ellis, or 'dogs' who betrayed their fellow prisoners, as in Henry Belfield's murder of Thomas Boardman, who may have caused his removal to the settlement.[17]

In 1841, William Derrincourt was undergoing a sentence to stonebreaking when Patrick Minehan battered James Travis with a hammer after they had finished breaking stones and were returning to the penitentiary. Derrincourt was relieved that he was not present at the time, otherwise he might have been named as an accessory: 'however, I found that the men on either side of Travis had only been taken to Hobart as witnesses and had been glad of the trip'. After the assault, an overseer named Simcock immediately ran towards Minehan and said

' "Paddy, you should not have done that." ' He replied, ' "There lies one b——y dog, stiff enough." ' Minehan was tired of life, he said, and he believed that Travis, who died shortly afterwards in the hospital, deserved what he got.

At the trial, the prisoner and the six witnesses from the settlement were called 'most unfavourable, not to say repulsive specimens of humanity' by the *Hobart Town Courier*. During the trial, Minehan was restless, objected to the evidence of two of the prisoners, said they would not have been permitted to give evidence in England, and claimed he was as innocent as anyone in the court. Six months earlier, Minehan had been sentenced to death, but was reprieved. Now he was sentenced to be hanged and his body to be anatomized and dissected. ' "Thanks be to God, you cannot dissect my soul, although you can my body!" ' he exclaimed as he left the dock.[18]

The practice of ordering dissection after pronouncing the death sentence was not unusual, but six months after Minehan's trial the subject caused a lively controversy in Hobart, when the body of another Port Arthur murderer, Henry Belfield, was ordered to be handed over to Dr E. Bedford at the Colonial Hospital. Although nobody could deny that dissection was necessary in the interests of science, wrote the *Courier*, ordering dissection immediately after the death sentence was like taunting the condemned man. Dissection was all very well in its place, but it was being 'associated in the minds of the multitude with the violent death of malefactors and assassins'. Consequently, many people in extreme poverty were reluctant to seek medical help and chose instead 'to expire in their own hovels, deprived of every comfort'.[19]

In Hobart, dissections were carried out at the hospital, but Port Arthur's hospital also had a dissecting-room, about which little is known. The convict, Linus Miller, whose duties as church clerk involved him with burials at the settlement, wrote: 'When a prisoner died, his remains were dissected, [and]

In the early years, if a prisoner died at Port Arthur his body was dissected, before burial on the Isle of the Dead. Later, the dead were apparently first taken to the church from the hospital, from where this photograph was taken, and then to the island.

put into a rough coffin in a state of *perfect nudity*, (even the shirt in which they die are stripped off!)'.

The 'horrible frequency' of violent crimes at Port Arthur worried the authorities, so much so that in 1845 Judge Algernon Montagu considered having the murderer, Francis Maxfield, returned to the settlement and hanged in chains as an example to the other prisoners. Instead, at the exact time of Maxfield's death, the men were assembled for prayer and a sermon, and apparently this procedure continued for some years.[20]

Henry Belfield battered another Port Arthur prisoner mercilessly because he suspected Thomas Boardman had caused his removal to the settlement. Belfield was described as 'a poor, simple, well-featured boy' before his hanging at Hobart.

8 The Separate Prison and the Penitentiary

In 1842, the 'separate system' of prison discipline, which had been developed in Philadelphia in the United States in the late 1830s, was put into practice at the newly completed Pentonville Prison in England. This huge prison featured silence and separation of one prisoner from another in 'apartments' or cells, and became known as The Model. The system was soon adopted in Tasmania, but in a modified way. To Lieut.-Governor Denison it seemed an ideal method of dealing with the prisoner who continued to commit crimes and knew that nothing more could be done to him than send him back to Port Arthur, where he would undergo the same routine of discipline again.[1]

Denison proposed to build separate apartments at Port Arthur, he advised his superiors in London in 1847, and to confine men in strict solitude for periods varying from a year to eighteen months: 'for by this system only do I anticipate any chance of relieving the colony from a permanent class of offenders—men who have no sooner paid the penalty of one crime than they are sure to commit another.'[2] Elsewhere in the colony separate apartments already existed, and by mid 1848, 100 hurriedly and poorly constructed wooden and brick separate apartments had been built at the settlement.[3]

Port Arthur's first separate apartments were not as successful

as they might have been; although the wooden walls had brick infilling, they were not thick enough to prevent communication among the prisoners in the ten passages. From this primitive separate prison grew the idea of a prison on a grander scale, in stone, and modelled on Pentonville. Meanwhile, the old barracks or penitentiary, which had been temporary for so long, became even more shaky and dilapidated, and Commandant Champ's pleas for a new building remained unanswered (like those of Booth) until long after he left the settlement in 1848.

Port Arthur's separate prison was begun in 1848 and completed in 1852. Like Pentonville, its aims were instruction and probation, rather than oppressive punishment, such as flogging, and the prisoner was urged to reflect on the privations he was suffering as punishment for crime. In England, the 'separate system' was defined as a discipline 'in which each individual prisoner is confined in a cell, which becomes his workshop by day and his bed-room by night, so as to be effectively prevented from holding communication with, or even being seen sufficiently to be recognized by a fellow-prisoner'.[4]

The 'utmost vigilance' was used to deprive the prisoners of seeing each other's faces. According to the Pentonville authorities:

each prisoner, when out of his cell for any purpose, wears his cap with the peak down, which is sufficiently large to cover his face as low as the mouth ... So entirely has this arrangement answered the purpose, that we have no reason to believe that, since the opening of the prison—a period of 15 months—a single instance has occurred of one prisoner having seen the countenance of another. ...[5]

A rare, early view of the separate prison before the asylum was built to its right. The photograph dates from the early 1860s and is the work of Samuel Clifford, who began business in 1859. He used a horse-drawn, dark-room caravan, as did some other photographers of the time.

The separate apartments at Pentonville, unlike cells for solitary confinement, were fitted with 'every convenience to ensure ventilation, warmth, cleanliness, and personal exercise. Whatever is necessary to the preservation of the prisoner's well-being, moral as well as physical, is strictly attended to'. In solitary confinement, a man was placed in any type of cell, fed only on bread and water, and deprived of contact and conversation with all humans, whereas in a separate apartment he was fed nourishing food and kept apart from other prisoners but had limited contact with the staff.[6]

In every respect, except its size, the separate prison at Port Arthur—or The Model, as it came to be known—resembled Pentonville, including the size and design of the apartments and their fittings, which were imported from England. The prison, which is now partly restored, is built of stone, with some brick work. Fifty cells, arranged in three wings, radiate from a central hall, from which each wing can be seen, and the fourth wing contains the chapel with fifty separate wooden stalls. The prison had baths with hot and cold water. A kitchen and staff quarters were included, and from the head keeper's house nearby, there was an underground gutta-percha (rubber) tube to enable him to communicate with the duty officer at night.[7]

There were four exercise yards, one of which was for convicts who had been moved to one of two dark or dumb cells for a few days as severe punishment. No sound or light could penetrate these cells, which were small and cold with windowless walls nearly a metre thick, and were entered through an outer door and three inner doors.[8] 'When the outer door alone is closed, the interior is perfectly dark', reported the Hobart *Mercury*, 'and the loudest shout is barely distinguishable.

A convict at Pentonville Prison, England, wearing the mask featured as part of the 'separate system'. The mask was adopted at Port Arthur and the prisoner never left his cell without putting it on.

But when all four are shut, a prisoner might bawl himself hoarse and the sound would fall on no ears but his own. To call this cell gloomy would come far short of the reality'.[9]

The 'separate system' was genuinely believed to be humane and enlightened. At all times, the regulations required the head keeper of the Port Arthur prison to 'show the utmost forbearance and humanity' to its inmates and ensure that the staff did the same. 'Upon no account will he permit the convicts to be treated harshly or with violence, nor suffer any reproachful or irritating language.' These requirements contrast strangely with the rigidly maintained solitude, the eerie masks with slits for the eyes, and the use of the grim dumb cells.[10]

When a new prisoner was admitted to the prison, his leg-irons were removed, he was searched, bathed, given a hair-cut, and dressed in grey clothing marked with the letters SP (separate prison). His brass cell badge, on which was a number, was attached to the left side of his jacket, and from then on he was never addressed or referred to by his name. Before leaving for his cell, he donned a cap with a large peak that formed the mask, which, like his badge, he wore only when outside the cell. All his possessions were stored until his discharge.

In *The Criminal Prisons of London*, Henry Mayhew observed that the peculiar brown cloth cap and mask worn at Pentonville Prison gave a kind of tragic solemnity to the prisoners, and nothing about them appeared vulgar and brutal, but when they removed the masks, they were ordinary, coarse-featured men. The masks, designed originally so that the men's faces would not be seen in their shame, seemed to Mayhew to be merely a piece of 'wretched frippery' and as useless as they were theatrical.

A decade after Pentonville was built, the authorities concluded that the masks did not prevent prisoners from

The separate prison plan.

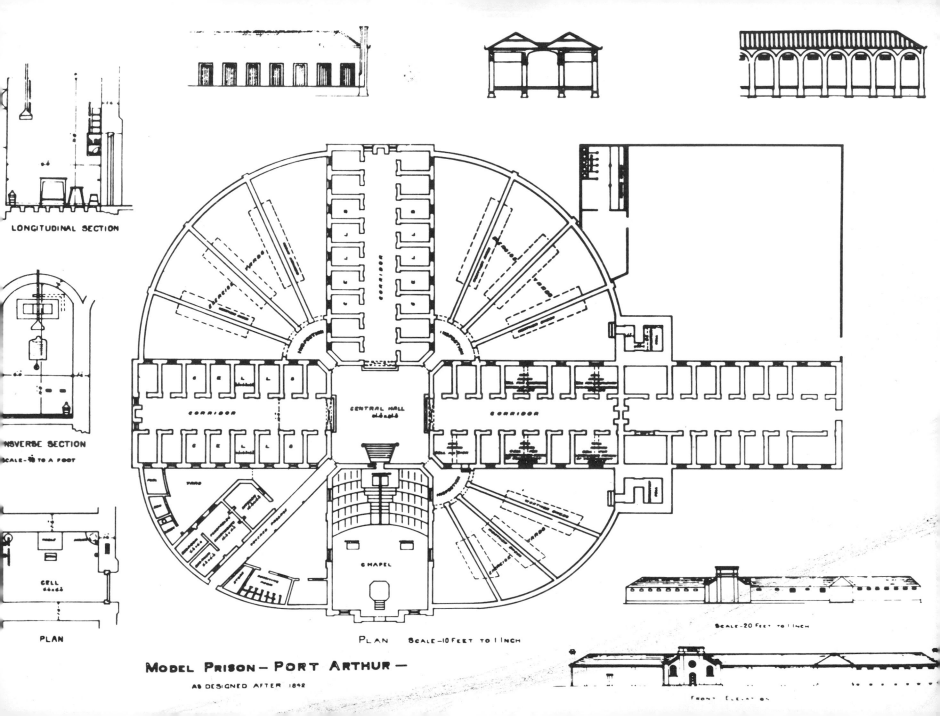

LONGITUDINAL SECTION

TRANSVERSE SECTION

SCALE—⅛ TO A FOOT

CELL

PLAN

PLAN   SCALE—10 FEET TO 1 INCH

SCALE—20 FEET TO 1 INCH

FRONT ELEVATION

MODEL PRISON — PORT ARTHUR —

AS DESIGNED AFTER 1842

CORRIDOR

CENTRAL HALL

CORRIDOR

CELLS

CHAPEL

recognizing each other in the prison: 'moreover, that as prisoners see each other before they are brought to the prison, come in considerable bodies, and are assembled together when they leave', it was desirable to abolish the masks. Also, they 'depressed the spirits of the men, without obtaining any corresponding advantage'.[11]

In the same year, Port Arthur's separate prison was built, described as 'this monument of official stupidity' by Marcus Clarke, and the masks were introduced and worn until the settlement closed in 1877.[12] They were introduced to Pentridge Prison in Victoria by William Champ after he left Port Arthur, and continued to be used in some British prisons.

Once the new prisoner reached his cell, he was allowed to remove the mask. Now he had a clear view of his cell for the first time, the workshop and bedroom in which he would spend up to twelve months or more. It measured about 1.8 by 2.8 metres and was 3.3 metres high, with a small barred window through which he was not permitted to look. There was a table, a stool, a rolled-up hammock on one of the shelves, books, basin, towel, eating utensils, and, as there was no gas or fittings for a lavatory, a lamp and a covered night-tub were provided. The use of the bell-pull was explained to the prisoner—he could ring it in urgent circumstances and an officer would reply promptly.

No longer was speech a regular part of the convict's daily life. He was never 'to read aloud, sing, whistle or dance', according to the regulations hung on the whitewashed cell wall. In this thick-walled prison, the sound of bells, the ticking of a clock, the swish of brooms when the men cleaned their cells or the corridors, the soft footfall of the slippered staff at night, and prayers and singing in the chapel must have come as a welcome relief. On the other hand, the prisoner was visited twice weekly by the medical officer, who examined him and if necessary recommended a relaxation of discipline or an increase in food,

A cell in Pentonville Prison. The Port Arthur separate prison cells or 'separate apartments' were designed on the same plan and the fittings imported from England. Tailoring was the main occupation at first for the Port Arthur separate prison men.

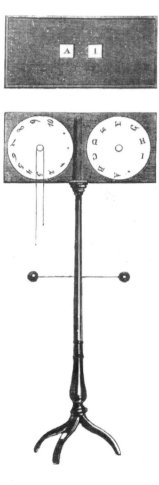

bedding or clothing, and the magistrate also visited and enquired if there was any complaint. Other staff, including the chaplain, schoolmaster and trade instructor, called regularly.

The regulations left nothing to chance. When meals were delivered, for example, two officers and two constables were present. The constables carried the meals, while one officer unlocked the trap-door of the cell and the other passed the meal through. No more than four trap-doors were ever unlocked at the same time, and doors opposite one another in a wing were never opened together, to avoid any chance of communication among the men. If a prisoner complained about the quantity of his food, it was weighed in the presence of another; if he said the food was unwholesome, it was exchanged. The food was similar to that served to other prisoners at Port Arthur, although during the first two months in the separate prison the men received half rations. Many men were also admitted to the prison for solitary confinement on bread and water followed by 'separate' treatment.[13]

Towards the end of the settlement's history, when discipline had relaxed somewhat, Mark Jeffrey or 'Big Mark', whose preoccupation with food seemed to be unceasing, was confined in the prison. Jeffrey had been at Millbank Prison in England, where he was remembered as 'the most daring ruffian', according to Mayhew; he was ultimately transported for life for assault. In the 1870s, when he was serving a second life sentence for manslaughter committed four years earlier, he made a request that was altogether without precedent in the prison's history, if not that of the settlement's.

'Mark Jeffrey has just asked me to send him a dinner, today being the Queen's birthday', wrote the Reverend Rowland Haywood to the Commandant, Dr John Coverdale. 'I should esteem it a great favour if you would kindly give me leave to do so.' As Port Arthur was likely to be closed by the Queen's next birthday, in 1877, Coverdale was unwilling to oppose the request, he told the chaplain, but possibly he was taking the line of least resistance, as Jeffrey was a troublesome old reprobate who tried the patience of the staff to the utmost. No doubt Haywood, who was one of the most hard-working staff and carried out his duties 'in a spirit of cheerfulness and hope', supplied the dinner from the kitchen of the parsonage.[14]

Daily, the prisoners put on their badges and caps, pulled down the masks, and left their cells for an hour's exercise in the yard. When the officer called ' "Walk about" ', each man, facing the wall, turned up his mask and briskly exercised. (In hot or wet weather they were under shelter.) Five times a week the men again left their cells, to attend the chapel, when they mounted the stairs leading from the central hall into their stalls. (Catholics and Protestants attended at different times.) Once inside his stall, the prisoner shut the door, raised his mask and hung his badge on a hook. When the row was filled, an officer closed the outer door and, simultaneously, with a locking-bolt, locked all the doors in the row. After the service, the order in which the convicts were to leave was indicated silently by letters and numbers on a signalling device.

The chapel of a separate prison was said to be the place for communication among the convicts. Henry Mayhew described several methods of communicating. One man might leave a note in a stall as he passed it to reach his own, or push a note under his door, or even over the top (when he might easily be seen by the officers sitting on elevated seats at the front). A short, abrupt cough would attract the attention of a neighbour. Prisoners also used a code with a number of raps with the knuckles representing a letter of the alphabet—a tedious but effective method that enabled them to learn a good deal about each other.

The signalling device in the chapel at Pentonville Prison, and also at Port Arthur.

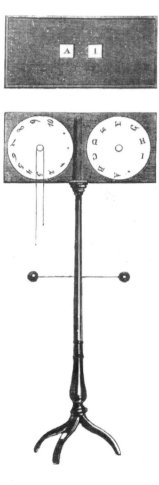

INTERIOR OF MODEL CHAPEL - PORT ARTHUR. 479.A.

The separate prison chapel at Port Arthur after the settlement was closed in 1877. The prison was gutted by fire in 1895.

Prisoners during a chapel service at Pentonville Prison. Once inside their stalls, the men were permitted to remove their masks.

By day each cell was a workshop. At first, tailoring was the main occupation, but within a few years the range of activities extended. In 1862, the products included canvas jackets for the mentally ill, flags, braces, pads for leg-irons, lining for prison masks, mattresses, brooms, baskets, mats, rugs and shoes. From the mid 1860s, some prisoners were permitted to work together in areas that had been adapted as a workshop.[15] In the evening some convicts read books before bedtime and Frederick Mackie met several men who had memorized whole chapters of the Bible. At 8.30 p.m., a bell was rung. Hammocks were unrolled and the hooks at each end were inserted into rings in the wall. The workshop had become the bedroom.

The prisoners were expected to keep themselves and their cells clean and tidy. They washed their feet twice weekly in summer in the evenings before they put on a clean shirt, and once a week in winter, and they repaired their own clothing. If ever one convict had to pass another outside their cells, the one to be passed immediately faced the nearest wall until the other was about 4 metres past him. In the presence of the officers or visitors, the prisoners had to show the utmost respect and touch their caps.

In 1849, before the separate prison was completed, eighteen cells were occupied by a group of prisoners destined for Norfolk Island. Their behaviour in ordinary cells in Hobart had been so ungovernable that it was unsafe to approach them, but after experiencing the isolation of the Port Arthur prison, they very quickly became quiet and orderly, and it was thought that the separate prison and the penal settlement on the island would be powerful means of restraining them.[16] The worst class of convicts were placed in the prison: those under very heavy

B wing of Port Arthur separate prison. Complete silence was maintained and the staff wore slippers.

The restored stairs leading to the separate prison's chapel. There is a spy hole in the heavy door.

The asylum, left, and the separate prison.

Part of the restored ceiling of the asylum's dining hall.

The guard house and tower, built in 1835.

Above left
The restored chapel of the separate prison. Each prisoner had a separate stall.

Left
The ruin of the church nestles among trees.

sentences, desperate characters who had spent years in gaol in Britain, and those who had committed indecent acts. After four to twelve months, the most violent and disobedient were expected to be subdued.[17] As the separate prison was so dreaded, cells were always available as a deterrent to men who might consider absconding or other serious crimes.

In the separate prison, some of the men had scarcely known what freedom was, having been in prisons from their youth, according to Frederick Mackie. He visited men who wept because they were unused to kindness from a stranger, and when prisoners were brought out of the dumb cells to see him, he was 'pained with their half frightened, half bewildered look as they removed the cap which covers the head and face'.

While a number of reports written by visitors to the prison dwelt on its sensational aspects, the missionary gave a more balanced view. He described most of the men in it at the time as young men transported as 'mere boys' to Point Puer, across the bay. Most of them were in the prime of life, had good natural ability, and if their energies had been properly directed they might have been useful and notable.

Mackie described a man who was between thirty and forty years of age and had been transported at the age of eleven. A stout, powerful man, he had an 'intelligent commanding countenance, with a keen piercing eye', and might have been 'great and noble':

The eloquence of nature was infused into his words and manner, as he spoke of his ardent breathings for liberty. Brought up and educated in prisons as he and many more have been, their mental constitution becomes different to that of other men, they have associations, habits and ideas which belong only to themselves. By this time he had obtained some indulgence, being allowed full rations, and having a little employment. He was making a worsted mat for the prison.

According to the writer Anthony Trollope, in *Australia*, one of the heroes of the place was an Irishman, Dennis Dogherty, who had been transported in 1833 for desertion from the army and was sentenced to life imprisonment four times after his arrival. The fourth occasion was at Oatlands in Tasmania for assault, being armed with a gun, and 'putting another man in bodily fear'. The death sentence was commuted to penal servitude for life, and in February 1872, when Trollope spent 'two very pleasant days' at Port Arthur, Dogherty was in the separate prison after an escape attempt.[18]

From Dogherty, Trollope learnt that the convict had not been free for one hour in forty-two years and in that time he had received nearly 3000 lashes. A large, powerful man, he claimed that he was broken, and with kindly treatment 'would be as a lamb'. But within the past few weeks he had escaped with three others and was brought back to Port Arthur nearly starved to death. 'The record of his prison life was frightful', wrote Trollope. 'He had been always escaping, always rebelling, always fighting against authority—and always being flogged . . . there he stood, speaking softly, arguing his case well, and pleading while the tears ran down his face for some kindness, for some mercy in his old age.'

When Dogherty said ' "I have tried to escape—always to escape—as a bird does out of a cage" ', Trollope was so touched that he wished he could have taken the convict 'out into the world, and given him a month of comfort', but in all probability, he said, he would have 'knocked my brains out on the first opportunity'. The staff assured the writer that Dogherty was 'thoroughly bad, irredeemable, not to be reached by any kindness'. Despite his bad character, he was recommended for a ticket-of-leave in 1876.

Another Irishman in the prison was Daniel Ahern, whose appearance as described by Mackie was as revolting as Dogherty's was prepossessing. Like Dogherty, Ahern was large and powerful. He had come to the colony as a soldier, and in 1864 the death sentence for attempted murder of his wife was commuted to penal servitude for life. When Trollope saw him, he was a reformed character, busily making shoes. But for years Ahern's life had been 'absolutely the life of a caged beast—only with incidents more bestial than those of any beast'. He talked freely to Trollope about 'his little accident' with his wife. At the time, in 1872, this convict was expected to be under the closest surveillance for the rest of his life, but he was granted a ticket-of-leave when Port Arthur closed.

In 1860 a report in the *Advertiser* described some of the sights in the prison as 'harrowing in the extreme'. In some cells, men were 'pacing up and down with an aspect of the most determined ferocity—in others they were walking and indulging in a hideous grinning—some were standing in an attitude of mute despair'. The writer may have been describing men in part of C wing, which had been extended and modified in 1858 to accommodate some of the worst of the mentally ill. But even though James Boyd claimed the extension was excellent for 'peculiar cases of insanity', within months many of the cells had to be filled instead with desperados.[19]

In C wing, one of the most tragic and violent inmates was John Quigley, who had two cells converted into one, known as Quigley's Cage, and a private exercise yard. A labourer from Tipperary in Ireland, he had been transported to Sydney at the age of twenty-four, possibly for larceny. In 1843, Quigley received a life sentence for having firearms in his possession at Maitland in New South Wales and was transported to Tasmania. After a brief stay at Port Arthur, he was transferred to Norfolk Island, where his skull was fractured in a fight. He petitioned to be returned to the colony and left the island in 1849, only to be placed in the New Norfolk Asylum near Hobart. There, even though two boards of enquiry examined him and found he was insane, in 1852 he was discharged as a malingerer.

Three years later, in 1855, Quigley was charged with shooting a Mr Ritchie in the leg during an armed hold-up, and at the Launceston Gaol the convict was diagnosed by a Dr Casey as suffering from dementia, caused by the skull fracture. Quigley was so dangerous that before the trial Casey recommended that his hands should be handcuffed behind his back before the court appearance. According to the judge, the 'frightful wound' from the 'dreadful fracture' was still perfectly clear.

The jury returned the verdict that Quigley was a dangerous lunatic, so he was sent back to the hospital at New Norfolk, and from there to Port Arthur. He was described as a vicious, violent man with a cunning expression, and after the asylum was built there in the 1860s, he was one of the worst cases of the criminally insane. It was said that six or seven men were needed to handle him.[20]

Two years after Port Arthur's prison was completed, Boyd advised his superiors that solitary confinement on bread and water, followed by 'separate' treatment, was the most effective deterring and reformatory punishment and produced a decided improvement in the convict's future life. In the case of 250 men received from Norfolk Island, including some of the very worst in the British empire, the most violent men were behaving in a proper and rational manner.[21]

Until he left Port Arthur in 1871 Boyd regarded the prison as a most valuable part of the settlement:

the old, hardened prisoners, who have been flogged and chained until they have become morally and physically callous to bodily suffering and to any feeling of degradation, are perfectly subdued by isolation ... for I have invariably remarked, that when the worst prisoners are associated together the severest labour and heaviest chains are apparently but little feared; in like manner corporal punishment has often become the test of the convict's utter incorrigibility. It was a notorious fact, that the more unflinchingly a prisoner endured flogging the more he was looked up to ... and this mischievous flattery often led to the worst results. ... Such dangerous characters, however, dread seclusion; they cannot bear up under the working of their consciences; and ... are compelled to admit themselves humbled, and generally to plead for release. Such are the effects of solitary confinement, followed by separate treatment, as a punishment ... and there is good reason to hope that the majority ... do become at least outwardly reformed.[22]

If many were only outwardly reformed, others, according to Mackie, left the prison with 'good resolutions and with desires to amend', but he also made the pertinent observation that they soon mingled again with their 'evil associates'. He thought that if they were placed in 'a respectable community', in other words, not in Tasmania, which was filled with convicts and ex-convicts, 'separate' treatment might have far-reaching results.

The isolation of the separate prison had other far-reaching results. Long periods of isolation would have precipitated serious and sometimes permanent mental illness among these men, a proportion of whom were sociopathic personalities vulnerable to mental illness. Even the most stable would have been affected by the deprivation of contact. The number of men who were transferred from the prison to an asylum will not be known until the record of every prisoner who was sent to the colony is examined and the Port Arthur men's records isolated. Even then, the records will show only those 'lunatics' diagnosed in the light of medical knowledge of the times.

Nor will the number of suicides and attempts at suicide in the separate prison, and at Port Arthur generally, be discovered until the records are studied. In 1872, there was a suicide attempt in the prison, recorded by an officer, George Whittington, in his report for 1871–2. He had 'no irregularity or special occurrence' to report, except one, which he underlined: 'John Brown per *Eliza* an inmate of the Separate Prison attempted suicide by cutting his throat and arms with a knife he was using while employed at shoemaking'. Brown (alias Newby) was forty-five years old and was serving a four-year sentence at Port Arthur.[23] In his lengthy annual report, the medical officer, Dr E. C. McCarthy, neglected to mention Brown.

In 1853, Mackie described a convict who was thought to be a malingerer by the doctor and who perplexed the staff. The man was 'apparently in a lethargic state, sitting on his stool with his head sunk down upon the table. He made no motion, he spoke not a word'. The officer with Mackie lifted the man and stood him against the wall of the cell. 'We endeavoured to elicit something from him but in vain, nothing escaped him but a shuddering groan and he seemed ready to sink upon the floor.' He had been in this condition for a month or so, but staff, observing him through the spyhole in his cell door, had sometimes seen him exercising 'when he might suppose he was not seen'. Despite the doctor's opinion, James Boyd thought the prisoner should be removed from 'separate' treatment.

Although Boyd was obviously not a callous man and had the welfare of the prisoners at heart, after observing the effects of isolation in the prison for eighteen years, he still believed firmly in its advantages, as did his superiors. The Comptroller-General of Convicts, W. Nairn, wrote in a report that it was impossible 'to over-estimate the value of this mode of treatment', providing 'its operation is carefully watched so as not to produce injurious effects on the health or mental state of the Prisoners and when the periods of detention are kept within moderate limits'. By the use of 'separate' treatment, plots for escape or other offences were avoided, as well as 'severe' punishment.[24]

But the commandant from 1874 to 1877, Dr John Coverdale, had different ideas about 'separate' treatment and in 1875 he told a Select Committee on Penal Discipline that the isolation was 'decidedly injurious'. His view was supported by the chaplain, Rowland Haywood. Coverdale described the case of Leonard Hand, who had been convicted of an indecent offence at the age of fifteen in 1866. For three years—not continuously—Hand had been in strict isolation, 'and the effects were not good physically or morally. He is now mentally childish and silly, but at the same time mischievous'. Haywood told the committee that 'separate' treatment was 'very hurtful to the mental powers, especially with young men' like Hand, whose condition had deteriorated over the eighteen months he had observed him.

Despite a regulation that clearly stated that if the mind of a convict appeared to be affected the medical officer and chaplain were to be notified, Hand had continued to languish in his cell, although Coverdale and Haywood were obviously concerned about him. Their evidence was contradicted by a former head keeper of the prison, George Whittington, who thought Hand was 'just what he was when he came here'—in 1866 at the age of fifteen—'he was always looked on as very bad, and he is just the same now. No better nor worse than he ever was.' When the Roman Catholic chaplain, the Reverend W. R. Fitzgerald, gave evidence, he agreed that Hand's health was worse, but his incarceration was 'expedient'. No doubt the confinement of Thomas Meaghan, who had been convicted of rape at the age of fifteen, was also expedient, even though the chaplain said there was 'no escape from lunacy' for him if he was kept much longer in the prison.[25]

At the time the committee met, there were eighty-nine convicts at the settlement, which was nearing its end. Twenty-two of the men were 'bad, very bad, dangerous, and either convicted [of] or suspected of unnatural vice', thirty-two were 'likely to become a public charge through inability to earn a living, or by invincible propensity to theft, forgery, &c. &c.', and there was hope for the remaining thirty-five. Seven of the men were in the separate prison, including Leonard Hand, whose character was 'indifferent', Daniel Ahern ('a slight improvement on very Bad'), and Mark Jeffrey ('bad').[26]

Appalled by the prisoners' old barracks or penitentiary that he saw at Port Arthur in the mid 1840s, the social reformer, the Reverend Henry Phibbs Fry, wrote scathingly in *A System of Penal Discipline* of not one building built of brick or stone for the convicts. In his opinion, the materials used for an ornamental and unnecessary soldiers' barracks surrounded by a high, long brick wall, and the tower of the church, could have provided substantial accommodation for all the men, yet they still slept and ate their meals in dilapidated, over-crowded, wooden 'dens'.

The prisoners' huts were more extensive then than they had been, and had been added to when necessary. In 1846, they were situated in four yards within the stockade and contained 894 bunks. Considering the poor buildings the discipline was as good as it could be, Commandant Champ reported to his superiors, and a new penitentiary was all that was needed 'to render the settlement, as a place of punishment, as efficient as such an establishment can be expected to be'.[27]

Before Champ left the settlement in 1848, all prisoners had been set to work to convert the existing huts. For the better surveillance of the men at night, partitions had been removed, leaving long ranges of bunks separated from one another by wooden rails. One of the huts had become a mess-room. Elsewhere in the colony, similar conversion had been carried out in convict sleeping quarters in an attempt to avoid 'unnatural crime', as was the case at Port Arthur. But nothing more was done at the settlement, apart from constructing the primitive separate apartments and beginning the separate prison, although the possibility of using the four-storey mill and granary as a penitentiary was discussed.[28]

By the time the separate prison was completed in 1852 and a wing of it extended in 1853, the mill and granary—believed to be 'the largest edifice in the colony'—was long overdue for conversion, which was begun in September 1853. The work was 'pushed on with much energy' and took precedence over

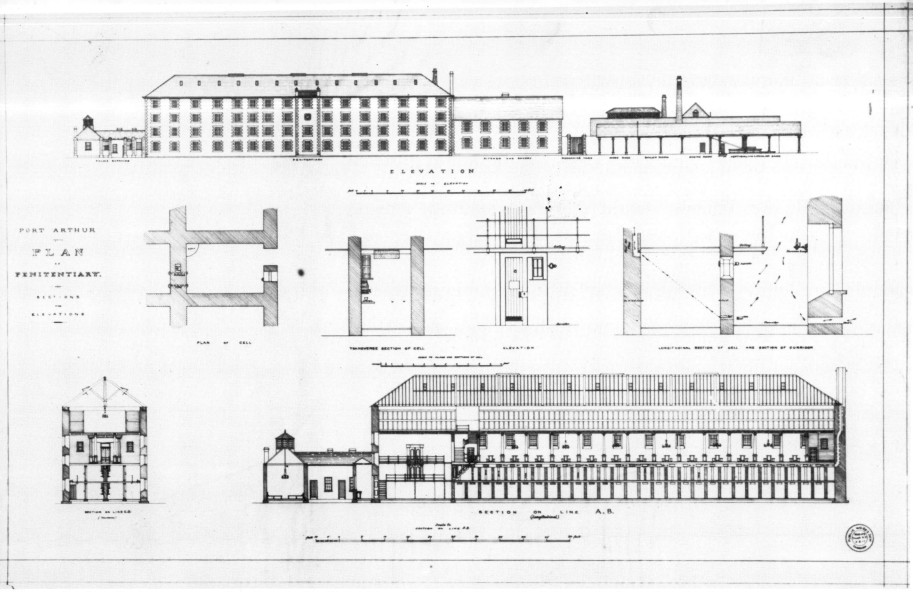

A plan of the mill and granary as converted into the penitentiary. The two tiers of cells are on the first and second floors, the dining-room (showing tables, benches and over-hanging lamps) on the third, and the dormitory on the top floor. In the latter, the bunks were separated by wooden rails.

all other at Port Arthur until it was completed and occupied in 1857. Within a few months, by January 1854, 136 separate apartments, on the same plan (though smaller) as those in the separate prison, were finished.

These cells formed two tiers in what had been the first and second storeys. In each tier the cells were arranged in a double row, back to back, with their doors facing to the outer walls of the building. The furnishings were the same as those in the prison, and most of the cell fittings and all the locks, bells and fluted glass were imported from England. Galleries with neat railings were constructed in front of each row of the upper tier, and meals could be trundled along each gallery on a 'railway carriage', and delivered through the trap-door of each cell.[29]

When the conversion was completed, at one end of the cells there was a lofty, handsome entrance hall, extending to above the second tier and lit by an equally handsome kerosene chandelier. Kerosene lamps were also hung in the corridors. (Boyd had hoped to have gas lighting, which was introduced in 1857 in the Hobart penitentiary, because it was cheap and clean. Gas had been made experimentally at the settlement in 1854.) The galleries around the hall also had railings, and wooden staircases rose to the upper tier of the cells and above to the next storey, where the dining-room was situated.[30]

A wide staircase led to the spacious dining-room. On the right of the landing was the pantry, which contained rows of tin plates and pannikins; to the left was the library. Green drapery divided the landing from the dining-room, which measured a little more than 49 metres long and nearly 10 metres wide. Plain, slender columns supported the ceiling, from which hung kerosene lamps to light the rows of tables and benches. To save time and labour, a lift worked by a windlass hauled food up from the kitchen below. On this floor there was a room for school lessons, and a Roman Catholic chapel. The chapel's appointments were said to be miserable in the extreme, which could easily be explained if only prisoners used the chapel, but the free population also worshipped there.[31]

On the top floor, above the dining-room, was the dormitory, which was nearly 70 metres long and 10 metres wide. It was originally intended to have 604 bunks in three tiers, but because the settlement's population had decreased, only 348 were required in two tiers.[32] 'The dormitory was like nothing so much as the 'tween decks of some huge ship', wrote Marcus Clarke in 1870 after a visit to Port Arthur. 'The bunks were railed off [from each other], and the convicts lay with their heads to the ship's side. Lamps were kept burning through the night, and a watchman patrolled the space between the berths.'[33] In 1871, the dormitory also had some iron bedsteads (and by then it had 228 vacant bunks). There were twenty-two lavatories, and ten baths with hot and cold water, although the prisoners tended to regard cleanliness as 'a sort of refined punishment'.[34]

On a turret on the front of the building a large clock ticked. Facing it was a stone wall, in which there was an ornate stone drinking fountain made by one of the convicts. At the back of the building there were more lavatories, exercise yards with covered verandahs, fixed seats, and fire-places to warm the prisoners in wintry weather. A shed nearby housed two fire-engines, and twenty-four neat-looking helmets hung on the wall. Adjoining the penitentiary were the constables' and watchmen's barracks, the kitchen, bakery, clothing store, laundry and hot-air drying rooms. The many nearby workshops included the sawmill, sawpits, timber store and stone-cutters' shed, some of which were near completion in 1857, and others were underway. A new flour mill, to be powered by a steam engine, was also being built.[35]

The dining-room of the penitentiary, photographed some time after Port Arthur was closed in 1877.

The dormitory of the penitentiary.

According to enthusiastic visitors who inspected the building, the penitentiary surpassed all others. 'It promises, ay, and at no distant period, to be as effective a receptacle for prisoners as any penitentiary in Europe', the colony's Crown Solicitor, Edward McDonnell, wrote in the settlement's visitor's book in 1855. A member of parliament thought the building would be 'one of the most complete and admirably arranged gaols in the empire'.[36] And the *Mercury*'s report of March 1870 positively glowed. The penitentiary's appearance was perhaps more imposing than that of any other public or private building in the colony, and the report continued:

its exterior has the appearance rather of an immense warehouse, surrounded by many workshops, than that of a prison. Its interior better represents a mansion.... Its magnificent staircase, its carpeted passage, its burnished bannisters, its snowy white floors, its well ventilated dormitories, its magnificent dining-room, its well appointed kitchen, its hot and cold bath-rooms and smoking saloon ... all present an unexpected sight.

Towards the end of the conversion of the mill, the shallow part of the bay in front of the penitentiary and the church was reclaimed, giving ample space for the workshops and other purposes. But of the greatest importance was a new embankment, which prevented the sea from washing continually against the building and eroding the foundations. Already the sea and the poorly made bricks were having an effect, and the ravages of fire, and time, would in the future cause further damage.

9   Timber, Ships and Things

From the earliest days of the settlement, the sound of sawing and of falling trees rang through the thickly timbered bush for long hours daily throughout the year. Every morning the superintendent of convicts, who attended to the general management of the prisoners, mustered them, gave directions to the overseers or constables, and sent off the gangs to their work. At the evening round-up he received an account of the day's work, and next morning he presented it to the commandant. A weekly account was kept of the timber, shingles, and other products.

'Gentlemen' or educated convicts doing a little light work, at left, contrasted with the hard labour of a timber-carrying gang or, as it was often called, the Centipede.

Gangs of up to seventy men carried enormously heavy logs for long distances through almost impassable bush to the lumberyard, shipbuilding yard and sawpits at the settlement. A timber-carrying gang resembled 'a terrible colossal centipede crawling to attack you', the *Hobart Town Courier* reported colourfully in 1835. Two years later, the *Hobart Town Almanack* also described this labour, which 'has a wonderful effect in subduing refractory and turbulent spirits and is much dreaded by all'. The report continued:

Seen at a distance they look like an enormous centipede which they are sometimes called while moving along joined together as it were by the log itself for a backbone to which, like so many legs, they were severally attached. Self preservation compels every one to do his best

to support the immense weight, which … would crush him at once to death, whatever his efforts might be unless his companions in like manner did their part. This is considered the most severe labour on the settlement.

Until 1848, the overseers were convicts, who frequently abused their privileged position. Martin Cash wrote in *The Bushrangers of Van Diemen's Land* that he had known prisoners to be flogged and persecuted at Port Arthur for refusing to give up something as trivial as trouser braces to an overseer. 'I do not mean to say a prisoner would be flogged for refusing to give up his braces', he explained. 'I merely say that by so doing he incurred … displeasure, and this was a safe passport to the triangles.' (During a flogging, the man was strapped to a wooden structure shaped like a triangle.)

In his *Notes of an Exile*, the Canadian, Linus Miller, describes vividly his experiences in a timber-carrying gang and its overseer, whom he called 'Sawyer'. Miller was sure he could not endure 'the horrors of the "carrying gang" ' for long because he was already 'sadly emaciated and worn out'. Although he was an educated convict, he had been sentenced to severe labour at Port Arthur because he had absconded from a road party in the colony. One day the gang had to carry a huge log from the bush to the settlement and although he was the tallest man, he was forced to stand upright. The overseer, who had been transported for highway robbery, was a tyrant, and Miller was sure that Commandant Booth would have punished the man severely had he known of his behaviour. Miller recalled the orders the gang received from this man:

'Now, you bloody ——! I am going to teach you what Port Arthur is, and if any of you don't like the lesson, you have only to get a taste of the cat-o'-nine tails, and my bloody eyes! but you will fall in love with this business at once. Every man stand up straight when under it, if it drives his legs into the ground two feet.

Miller claimed he was nearly crushed to the earth several times by the weight of the log and had 'oaths and shameful abuse' showered on him not only by 'Sawyer' but by the other men, 'who at such times got their share of the load'.

Every week, the prisoners were checked by the medical officer to ensure that they were fit for the labour to which they were assigned, but men in the solitary cells were examined daily. Martin Cash wrote that the doctor was the first person at Port Arthur who had displayed the slightest feeling of humanity towards him. Linus Miller, after being in the carrying gang for several weeks, claimed that the heavy logs 'had so injured my chest that I was compelled to lean my head forward several inches; as standing upright, in a natural position, occasioned dreadful torture to my breast. My waistcoat and jacket, about the shoulders, were red and stiff with the congealed blood, from the wounds underneath'.

Perhaps Miller's description of his condition was slightly exaggerated, because he would have had a regular medical examination. After he had been in the carrying gang for five weeks, the doctor told him: ' "Miller, you look very ill. You cannot be able to perform such heavy work, and I shall shift you into the invalid gang." ' The convict's heart was 'too full to reply' and he burst into tears, the first he had shed at Port Arthur. He believed that another week in the gang would have ruined his health for life, or killed him outright. Miller received an absolute pardon in 1844, and by 1846 he had returned to the United States, where his book was published.

In contrast to Miller's account, John Frost's is more objective and lacks gory descriptions, although he was sentenced to hard labour in the quarries and a carrying gang. Frost was at Port Arthur at the same time as Miller. He had been Mayor of Newport in Wales, and was in a drapery and tailoring business. After being found guilty of treason as a Chartist, he was sentenced to be hanged, drawn and quartered, but the sentence was commuted to life transportation. He reached Hobart in

1840 and, like other political prisoners of the time, he was sent straight to Tasman Peninsula, given certain privileges, and worked in the commandant's office. He was granted permission by Booth to write a letter to his wife in England, but the letter was published there and displeased the authorities.

In consequence, Frost was sentenced to hard labour and in *The Horrors of Convict Life*, he wrote:

The commandant came to me one day after he had come from Hobart Town and said, 'I have orders to remove you from the office.' 'For what?' I asked. 'Have I conducted myself in a manner that is displeasing to you?' 'No,' said Captain Booth, 'you have given satisfaction.' 'And where are you going to put me?' inquired I. 'Why, I must put you in the gangs.' 'In the gangs, for what? Do you mean to put me in the gangs without trying me?'

I was kept in the gangs for two or three years, and subject to the very hardest kinds of labour that any man could endure.

Although Frost deplored the gangs as the heaviest kind of work, in contrast to Miller he claimed the work in the carrying gang 'did me no harm, it only raised my spirit, and I think that I was actually a stronger man after working in the quarries and carrying logs than I had been before. The exercise only added to my health, increased my strength, and increased my desire to try whether I could not be of some service to my fellow countrymen, if ever I should be permitted to revisit England'. Eventually, Frost did return to England, after receiving a conditional pardon in 1854.

When the timber nearest to the settlement had been felled, the prisoners penetrated hills and valleys, where vast trees and tree-ferns flourished. During a visit to the peninsula in 1853, the Quaker missionary, Frederick Mackie, came upon 'a complete wood of tree ferns' that reminded him of a Gothic crypt, 'the heads of the ferns forming pointed arches . . . in every direction, and the massive pillars well represented by the thick columnar

Huge blocks of stone at Port Arthur which were cut by convicts but never moved from the quarry.

A topman and a pitman sawing logs in nineteenth-century England.

stems of the trees. It was altogether an unique sight exciting astonishment and admiration'.

Mackie saw the timber-getters at work and an ingenious method used for conveying timber downhill: 'A ditch or channel is made down the sloping side of a hill: it is then lined with stout timber, put lengthwise. Down this huge groove the logs slide with great velocity and are thus brought into the neighbourhood of the mill.'[1] Later, in the 1860s, a similar shute of Norwegian design was constructed not far from Port Arthur. It was about half a kilometre in length and was supplied with logs from wooden or iron tramroads built by the prisoners and connecting with adjoining forests. Tramroads also carried logs to sawpits, where they were divided and conveyed to steam sawmills.[2] On the harbour, firewood and logs were conveyed to bush jetties and taken to the settlement by boat. The extensive wharfage there was eventually suitable for the colony's largest steamers and included a 5-tonne iron crane.[3]

Immense beams were carried from the bush to the ship-building yard, established in 1834 on a point jutting out to the east of the bay. There the work was said to be almost as difficult as the carrying gangs', and the men were frequently immersed in water to the neck.[4] Within a few years, the convict shipbuilders, who learnt the trade from a master shipwright, John Watson, or had already learnt it at Macquarie Harbour, produced a wide range of vessels. From 1834 until 1844 the prisoners built 4 schooners, 1 steam vessel, 2 lighters, 2 barques, 1 barge, 1 gunboat, 59 whaleboats, 3 tugs, and 88 other vessels, and in later years a few boats continued to be built and repaired.[5]

One of the earliest and finest ships constructed at Port Arthur was the *Eliza*, launched in 1835 and named after Lieut.-Governor Arthur's wife. A fast, armed schooner of 146 tonnes and valued at £2628, she was designed to patrol the Derwent River and Storm Bay, to intercept vessels leaving Hobart without paying port dues, and to prevent the escape of convicts by boat.[6] Launching an important ship was an occasion at the settlement, especially that of the *Fanny* in December 1837, because, at 282 tonnes and valued at £4544, she was the largest ship yet built in the colony. The barque was named after 'little Fanny Arthur', who at the time was sailing back to England with her family, after Arthur had been recalled.[7]

Soon after the *Fanny*'s launching, on 13 February 1838, when a small schooner was ready to set sail, the new Lieut.-Governor, Sir John Franklin, sent a message to the settlement advising that he wanted to name the boat after Booth. The commandant noted in his journal that the schooner 'gently glided into the deep'. Several years later, on 29 December 1841, 'a strong, staunch, wholesome-looking barque' of 276 tonnes was christened the *Lady Franklin* because Sir John's message requesting his wife's Christian name, Jane, had arrived too late.[8]

In *Old Convict Days*, William Derrincourt, who was involved with the construction of the *Lady Franklin*, wrote about his work:

In a few weeks I was told off to what was known as Morris's slip gang, and employed carrying knees, planks, and other timber for the building of a vessel called the *Lady Franklin*. When we had to remove a long heavy beam, all the bearers were ranked up on each side, and at the word 'lift', all hands laid hold and raised the beam shoulder high. The sub-overseer would then tell a number of men to step from under, leaving the rest to carry the burden, upon the top of which he would always ride.

If the prisoners tried to steady themselves by putting their hands on top of the beam for the ship, instead of at the sides, the overseer would give them 'severe and often damaging raps on the knuckles'. They carried the beams for a kilometre or more, and at times the weight was so great that their eyes were nearly

The Lady Franklin, *built by convicts at Port Arthur.*

forced from the sockets. New hands like Derrincourt suffered most because they were slow, and he was generally among the 'crawlers' who were particularly bullied by the overseer, who would threaten to leave him 'at the green door' (the commandant's office).

Port Arthur was essentially an industrial institution for decades and its workshops occupied the time of many prisoners, who also learnt trades that equipped them for life in the colony. An amazing quantity and variety of products emerged from the workshops for use at the settlement or for export to the colony, but the most important by far were timber products, as well as sawed timber. Millions of metres of timber were sawed for the settlement and for loading on to ships such as the *Charlotte*, *Derwent*, *Isabella*, *Penelope* and *Prince Leopold*. Sometimes two or three vessels would be anchored in the bay waiting to load. From 1830 to 1838—in only nine years—1.5 million metres of timber was cut, of which 600 000 metres were exported.[9] After Port Arthur's population decreased, the workshops began to concentrate on work for the settlement, and agriculture and horticulture became more prominent.

In the mid 1830s workshops were established for painters, carpenters, turners, wheelwrights, a tinman, a bookbinder, shoemakers, tailors and blacksmiths. As early as 1835, the authorities realized that the colonial boots and shoes were superior to the English variety, as was colonial leather, because leather imported for the shoemakers often deteriorated during the voyage or rotted on the Hobart wharves. Boots and shoes could be made at Port Arthur at half the price of the imported ones, and two pairs were issued annually there to each prisoner, whereas at other stations, three English pairs were issued, or more. In the 1840s, the number of shoemakers at Port Arthur was increased, and a tannery was established. The shoemakers became important not only to the economy of Port Arthur but

to the colony, which issued about 41 000 pairs of boots and shoes to male and female convicts in 1845 alone.[10]

Bricks, tiles, flowerpots and similar articles were produced by Port Arthur convicts by the early 1840s and, during a visit in 1842, David Burn went so far in his enthusiasm as to write that the pottery was superior. All that the convicts needed in order to create pottery 'a little inferior to Wedgwood's' was a pugmill for kneading the clay. Surviving examples of the pottery, such as tiles and pots, however, reveal that it was no threat to Wedgwood. Some interesting pieces are held by the Queen Victoria Museum and Art Gallery in Launceston, such as 'Good luck' plaques incised with verses, but these are said to be from a commercial pottery established after the settlement closed by a Mr Price, whose kiln near the settlement has been restored.

Brickmaking was an important activity for the prisoners, who not only provided them for use at Port Arthur, but for government works and for general sale in the colony. By the early 1830s, sun-drying of bricks had given way to firing them in kilns, which until about 1845 were situated south of the settlement, and later on a site to the north, now called Brickfields Hill. Sixty-eight thousand bricks were produced in March 1834; in December 1841 that number was more than doubled, and between 1858 and 1868, the average monthly production was 14 000 bricks. Some buildings in Hobart are probably made of Port Arthur bricks, and timber from the settlement was used in the building of the present Government House.

Scientific tests have revealed that many Port Arthur bricks were grossly underfired, and some were puddled with sea water and had a salt glaze. As fresh water was scarce at the settlement, there may have been no alternative to using sea water. Although seaspray could have caused the bricks to show a salt composition through accumulation, bricks taken from under the floor of a house at some distance from the sea also

A pair of child's shoes, to fit about an eight-year-old, made by a convict at Port Arthur.

A shoemaker in England in the nineteenth century.

The rear of the guard tower, which was built in 1835, showing ornamental ironwork made by convicts to hold a lamp.

show some saltiness. The quality of the bricks varied considerably and apparently deteriorated in later years. In 1876, the bricks sent to town for extensions to the Cascades Female Factory were, said Henry Hunter, 'of such a wretched and worthless description' that he refused to use them.[11]

While Charles La Trobe was acting as lieut.-governor in 1846–7, he visited the settlement and was welcomed, according to one of the officers, by 'poor old Lempriere in all his military glory' and Commandant Champ.[12] At this time there were nearly 1200 prisoners, many of whom were producing good work, which La Trobe inspected and reported on to his superiors:

The prisoners can perform almost every description of work. The workshops are excellent: very good locks, brass and iron castings, bells, taps, and dies of all sizes, lathes, scales and beams, and anvils are all made here, also boots. There were 58 shoemakers at work, one-half of whom were learners. The boots are cut out, examined, and given to the men, and are again examined when finished. Arrangements were in contemplation by which 250 pairs of boots will be made weekly. Between the months of April and November, 1846, 3000 pairs of boots of a superior description were forwarded from Port Arthur to Hobart Town.[13]

At about the time of La Trobe's visit, seventeen men worked in the large blacksmith's workshop. The furnace there could cast 5 tonnes of iron in one piece and nearly 560 kilograms of brass. Six forges were operating, and iron work for all government buildings, as well as Port Arthur, were wrought there. The peal of bells for the settlement's church had also been made in the foundry.[14]

By the late 1860s and the 1870s, the articles produced at Port Arthur began to reflect the changes there, not only of the type of men, but of the direction that production had taken. By this time a large proportion of the population was frail and old, including convicts, paupers, and the mentally ill. Some of the more unusual articles included blanket frocks, drawers, socks, stockings (none of which was worn by convicts), artificial arms and legs, crutches, a set of surgical instruments, a shower-bath (for treating the insane), shrouds and coffins. Coffins had always been made at Port Arthur, but the dead had not always been buried in shrouds.[15]

By the early 1850s, the importance of Port Arthur as an industrial institution and its contribution to the colony was well known in Tasmania. Now the work and talents of the prisoners began to be displayed at international exhibitions in London, Paris, Philadelphia and Melbourne. In 1851, for example, at London's Great Exhibition in the Crystal Palace, there was an immense plank of blue gum, 43 metres long from a tree 82 metres high, which had been felled by the prisoners.[16]

Again, in 1855, at the Paris Universal Exhibition, species of timber, possum and kangaroo skins, kangaroo skin shoes, an iron wheelbarrow, a kitchen roasting-jack, fire-irons, clays, bricks, tiles and flowerpots were displayed.[17] Pottery was also exhibited in 1866–7 at the International Exhibition of Australia, held in Melbourne, but no exhibits were more admired than the beautiful cabinet and ornamental woods prepared by the prisoners. The 117 items from Port Arthur included freestone quarried there, kangaroo, wallaby, possum and porcupine skins, seaweed, wheat, gig shafts, fancy walking sticks, hop poles. Five medals and eleven honourable mentions were awarded to the prisoners, although the work was always entered under the name of the commandant of the time and the location, Port Arthur.[18]

Ornamental polished wood was featured at the International Exhibition in Melbourne in 1875 and in the following year at the Philadelphia International Exhibition. (Apparently the same items were sent on from Melbourne to Philadelphia.) The work included twenty-four varieties of ornamental polished wood, and from Peter Carlsen—a free constable and wood-turner—there was a carved and turned spinning-wheel made of Tasmanian myrtle, a walking stick of sassafras, and a Danish pipe of ivory and myrtle.[19]

In 1862, one of the prisoners was gathering specimens— probably botanical—for the International Exhibition in London that year. At this time, the prisoner, Allan Williamson,

A large dispenser for soup or gruel used at Port Arthur.

The penitentiary, which was a mill and granary until the 1850s.

The commandant's simple house was extended to include an impressive entrance.

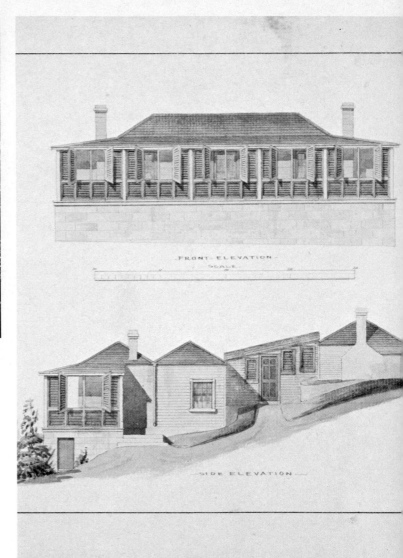

FRONT ELEVATION

SIDE ELEVATION

The front and side elevations, dated 1836, of the commandant's house.

who was a former gardener and land surveyor sentenced to Port Arthur for forgery, was knowledgeable about the varieties of ferns on the peninsula, and with the commandant's permission he roamed hills and gullies seeking rare specimens. He was frequently away from the settlement for days at a time. When he returned, he would dry, press, and name each specimen with 'all the accuracy of an accomplished botanist'. Williamson may have collected the specimens that were sent to the Government Botanist in Victoria, Baron Ferdinand von Mueller, in 1875.[20]

By the 1870s, the farm at Port Arthur consisted of stable, cowshed, piggeries, barns, stores, and dairies, and there were also farms nearby at Safety Cove, Long Bay and Garden Point. Agriculture and horticulture had increased in importance, as had fishing. Large quantities of salt, soap, milk and cheese were produced. In one year alone, about 5000 kilograms of salt, 11 000 litres of milk and 4000 kilograms of cheese were listed on official returns from the settlement, and in the 1870s, huge quantities of fish were caught. Fish was so abundant in the waters off Tasman Peninsula that the authorities' comparative disinterest in using this source of nutrition during much of Port Arthur's history is surprising, although security would have been a consideration. From an early date, however, fish was served regularly to hospital patients.[21]

The first fishery was established in 1848 by John Evenden, a Convict Department employee at Norfolk Bay near Port Arthur. He applied to the commandant for two well-behaved convicts to help construct the fishery at the mouth of a stream there, and later had about twenty others helping him. At each tide, immense quantities of freshwater mullet were enclosed in the fishery. Twice a week, six to eight railway waggons loaded with fish were sent to the settlement and boats collected loads for the coal mines and Eaglehawk Neck. In 1872, 2100 kilograms of fish were caught, but probably from areas other than Evenden's fishery.[22] By 1860, Evenden was permitted to run sheep and cattle in the Salt Water River area on the shores of Norfolk Bay for the settlement. There were also up to 600 deer roaming wild and destroying his crops, but the deer were protected and could not be shot.[23]

By the mid 1850s, most of the prisoners at Port Arthur worked on the task system that encouraged industry and good conduct, and featured the partial remission of sentences to those who deserved it. Other rewards included a little extra food for special industry or for working in wet weather, daily small allowances of tobacco, the gradual relaxation of heavy labour, employment in situations of comparative trust.[24] All the employment was intended to make the men useful to society after their discharge. According to the colonial authorities:

every man has the strongest incentives to conduct himself satisfactorily, in order to hasten his emancipation, and to enable him to participate in those high rates of wages and other great advantages now so common in the Australian colonies, and in which growing communities the man's former penal condition may not only be effectually concealed, but, if he be only steady and industrious, there is every reason to know that he will soon attain a respectable position in society.[25]

In 1862, a further improvement in conditions was introduced at the settlement in the form of small weekly money payments that depended on hard work and good conduct. When the payments were introduced, following a plan already adopted in Britain, the Comptroller-General of Convicts, W. Nairn, wrote:

It will of course be necessary to take care that the payments of money to the men … should be subject to such provisions as will prevent its being expended in drinking or otherwise under the influence of evil associates who may waylay prisoners known to be emerging from sentences with money in their possession.[26]

There were many talented tradesmen at Port Arthur and

The settlement in 1860 with a few people who are possibly convicts.

some worked hard to earn money. Had they kept to the straight and narrow after their release their trades could have been put to good use—and sometimes were. In 1863, the shipwright John Watson told a Select Committee on Prison Labour: 'When at Port Arthur I had under me several men who were classed as desperate offenders. With few exceptions I found them most willing to learn a trade, which some of them are now following in this and the neighbouring Colonies.'[27] From Watson's words emerges a rare insight into the lives of prisoners who succeeded, as opposed to those who continued with crime and remained a financial drain on the colony until their deaths in institutions.

The authorities hoped that those men who left the colony with money they had earnt would, after being away from their former evil haunts and associations, change their course in life. On the other hand, those who remained could subsist until they obtained employment. 'No man is now discharged from Penal detention penniless', it was said in 1863, 'and it must, therefore, be the Prisoner's own fault if any relapse into dishonest practices and habits'.[28]

When a man left Port Arthur, he returned to town by steamer, and was inspected at the wharf with a view to future identification. Until he found employment, he could get food and lodging at the penitentiary and be employed at stone-breaking.[29] Few felt inclined to take advantage of the offer and those who did soon left. Ticket-of-leave holders were generally allowed to choose where they wished to live, but some of the most desperate men, 'addicted to vices of a peculiarly revolting character', were ordered to remain in the town, where they were watched closely and visited by day and night at their homes.

After years at Port Arthur, prisoners found the surveillance unwelcome and some begged for permission to move to country districts, where they then committed outrages of 'painful notoriety'. Most of those who were released had careers of continuous crime. For example, in 1860, twenty-one men discharged from the settlement had records of crime extending over eight to thirty-one years, and averaging nineteen years. One was 'the worst character' in the colony.[30]

10   Escapes by Land and Sea

Throughout Port Arthur's history, prisoners made escape attempts by land and by sea in frail craft that were a tribute to their ingenuity and displayed desperation, determination and foolhardiness. Many men absconded, but few were successful in escaping from Tasman Peninsula. Sometimes they perished from starvation in the bush or by drowning. If they were caught, punishment was severe, yet some tried repeatedly to escape. After making their way back to the mainland of the colony, a few prisoners committed serious crimes and terrorized settlers, who lived in fear of escapees.

Despite the diligence of sentries at Eaglehawk Neck, prisoners still tried to escape by that route, by swimming or by canoe after the dogs were established. In the 1830s, Lempriere described a ludicrous attempt by a man named Billy Hunt, a former strolling player who adopted the disguise of a kangaroo and staged a performance that could only end in failure. As Hunt hopped towards the Neck, one of the sentries, who observed what he thought was a boomer (a large kangaroo), remarked, ' "I think I will have a shot at the boomer." ' To his surprise and amazement, the kangaroo answered, ' "Don't shoot, I am only Billy Hunt." ' Billy was captured and returned to Port Arthur, where his story probably amused officers and prisoners alike.

At first too few and too mild mannered, the dogs were eventually doubled in number, and in the 1850s there were eighteen chained across the Neck, on the surf beach of Pirates Bay and on platforms in Eaglehawk Bay. The dogs were frequently described as savage, and in the early 1840s had

'voices quite husky from continual barking', according to Captain Owen Stanley of the *Britomart*.[1] An example of their early ineffectiveness is given in Booth's journal in 1834. He was rather disgusted because the dogs had not barked as he walked past them, and the sentry in his box was far from alert. Soon the dogs became so well spaced across Eaglehawk Neck and so ferocious that no one would have been foolhardy enough to try to pass between them. A bold and resolute soldier attempted to, in the 1830s, and according to Lempriere he was severely wounded by the dogs.

In the 1850s the line of dogs, described by the Commandant, James Boyd, was 'as vigilant a body of sentinels as it is possible to imagine; many of them have not been off the chain for years, and are consequently very savage'.[2] The watch-dogs became renowned, not only in the colony but abroad. In his lively book, *Our Antipodes*, written after a visit to Eaglehawk Neck in 1851, Colonel Godfrey Mundy called the area 'one of the lions of Van Diemen's Land'. But Anthony Trollope, visiting Tasman Peninsula much later, in 1872, claimed he had thought the dogs were a myth until he saw them for himself, even though almost every author who described the peninsula, wrote of the dog guard in considerable detail, colourfully and sometimes inaccurately.

The already dramatic story of the dogs was irresistible to Mundy, who could not help embroidering it. He claimed that one of the dogs 'kept his teeth and temper in practice, by rushing into the shallows and fighting with the sharks; and he not infrequently succeeded in dragging them ashore'. Even

Commandant Boyd, who should have known better, referred to the sharks in his first official report to his superiors, but they had, it seems, encouraged the story in an attempt to deter prisoners from swimming across the bay.[3]

All the dogs had nicknames and were friendly only to those well-behaved convicts who were chosen to feed them. In the early 1840s, Harden S. Melville, the official artist aboard H.M.S. *Fly*, visited the area with Sir John and Lady Franklin, and wrote in his *Adventures of a Griffin*:

Those out-of-the-way pretenders to dogship were actually rationed and borne on the government books, and rejoiced in such sobriquets as Caesar, Pompey, Ajax, Achilles, Ugly Mug, Jowler, Tear'em, Muzzle'em.... There were the black, the white, the brindle, the grey, and the grisly, the rough and the smooth, the crop-eared and lop-eared, the gaunt and the grim. Every four-footed, black-fanged individual among them would have taken a first prize in his own class for ugliness and ferocity at any show. The animals could rub noses affectionately if they felt so inclined, but could not get sufficient hold of each other to have a fair mouthful, so, unless a collar or chain perchance gave way, fighting was out of the question. A fugitive would have to make a smart leap to clear danger, and even then of course the frantic baying and howling of the whole mastiff kennel would excite alarm....

The ladies of the party—with the exception of Lady Franklin, who possessed a nerve of steel—were naturally much alarmed at the violent straining of chains and the muscular and ferocious tension of excitement ... but misgivings on the score of personal safety were soon allayed by a little attenuated, swarthy Pole, also a convict, clad in a canary suit and leather cap.... He it was who trimmed their watch-lamps, brought their meat, shook up their beds, was their friend, and caressed them, and woe would have betided the assailant who hurt one hair of the little Pole's head....

After the dogs were well established, escapes were tried by way of the surf beach or the bay and there were attempts at disguise no more successful than Billy Hunt's but equally as ingenious. In an interview in 1927, for example, 80-year-old George Smith, described as Port Arthur's last living guard, told of a group of men who attempted to swim across Eaglehawk Bay with seaweed on their heads. (William Derrincourt related a similar story in *Old Convict Days*.) Smith described how a guard at Eaglehawk Neck was alerted when he noticed a peculiarly shaped bunch of seaweed:

'Hello,' he mused. 'That looks queer', but he did not attach any particular significance to it.... While he watched it, it would stay still on the surface, but ... it seemed to have an uncanny way of spurting ahead.... So he decided that he would turn his face away from it, but keep an exceedingly watchful eye on it just the same. Well, he did that, and he was amazed to see the thing quickly gather speed and glide along. He whipped round suddenly and it stopped.

He fired a shot and then another without effect. Then he pretended to leave the beach. He did not go very far before he suddenly swung around, when he was amazed to see that the weed had split into three pieces, each going at a great pace towards the opposite shore. So fast was the weed going, indeed, that it did not stop when he looked around, so he ran around to the spot where it was headed.... He did not have to wait very long....

'The cow's gorn,' he heard a voice say.

'Thank Mike,' he heard another. 'He dam' near got me that second time. I was just comin' up again.'

'Well, we'd better get orf for our lives now,' chimed in a third. 'Someone may 'ave heard the shots, an' be after us!'[4]

Smith's colourful story describes unsuccessful escapees, but the most enduring story of a successful escape by way of Eaglehawk Neck was that of the legendary Irish bushranger Martin Cash and his companions, George Jones and Lawrence Kavenagh. Each of the three men had been transported originally to New South Wales. They met at Port Arthur and after absconding, they hid in the bush for three days before setting off for Eaglehawk Neck, which they approached at dusk, and then swam across Eaglehawk Bay.

According to Cash's book, the most perilous part of their adventure was crossing the road that led to the Neck, where they might have been ambushed by guards. It was dark when they began their swim, and Cash soon lost sight of his mates. In the centre of the bay his clothes, which he had tied to his head, were washed away. When he reached shallow water he waited for Jones and Kavenagh, and eventually heard Jones say, ' "Martin's drowned" '. Cash sprang up to the bank, and the three men were amused to find that they had each lost their clothing during the crossing.

During the next few months the notoriety of Cash and company rested on their style of bushranging rather than on their escape. Although a few of their victims were not treated with the utmost consideration, Cash, the leader, usually managed to restrain his companions from violence and he became a story-book hero renowned for the gallantry he displayed to women victims. The three men roamed the colony together until Cash and Kavenagh were captured at Hobart. While they were on trial, Jones remained at large, joined two other escapees, and with the restraining hand of Cash lifted, he shot a constable and branded the legs of a convict woman with a red-hot spade. Jones was captured and hanged.

At the time of his trial, Cash enjoyed friendly visits from some of his victims. His cell was 'literally thronged with delicacies which had been sent to me by unknown parties', and the street between the gaol and the court-house was crowded with people determined to catch a glimpse of the gentleman bushranger. Both he and Kavenagh were fortunate enough to escape the death sentence and were sent to Norfolk Island. Nearly eight years after his arrival there, Cash was sworn in as a constable, as a reward for good conduct, whereas Kavenagh, who had committed murder, was executed.

Cash applied for permission to marry a convict woman, Mary Bennett, the servant of the doctor, and despite this audacious request, a marriage licence was sent to the island for them. After his release, Cash spent four years in New Zealand. He saved enough money to buy a farm at Glenorchy, near

Dogs chained to a platform in Norfolk Bay, on one side of Eaglehawk Neck, to give warning if convicts tried to swim across the bay.

Hobart, and there he lived—'known to all and enjoying the goodwill of all'—until the end of his life.

The gentleman bushranger achieved further fame in 1870, when with the utmost diffidence he was 'induced to appear before the public in the character of an Author', despite his illiteracy. The author of the widely read biography, which was first published as *The Adventures of Martin Cash*, was actually another convict, James Lester Burke, who received little credit for the authorship. Burke had been articled to a solicitor in Dublin before being court-martialled and transported for striking a sergeant of his regiment. Burke spent thirty-one years

Now Ready. Price One Shilling.

MARTIN CASH,

THE BUSHRANGER OF VAN DIEMEN'S LAND IN 1843.

A Personal Narrative of his Exploits in Company with Kavanagh and Jones, and his Experiences at Port Arthur and Norfolk Island.

TO BE HAD OF ALL BOOKSELLERS.

J. WALCH & SONS: WALCH BROS. & BIRCHALL.

Martin Cash's book, published in 1870, was first entitled The Adventures of Martin Cash *and was published by J. Walch and Sons of Hobart (a firm that is still in business, as is Birchalls, the booksellers, and the book's printer, the* Mercury*). By the late 1960s, some 32 000 copies had been printed by Walch's.*

in the colony and died on 24 July 1879 at the Brickfields Pauper Institute in Hobart.[5]

Martin Cash lived peacefully at Glenorchy and apparently his only brush with the law was when he was sixty-five years old. The incident was reported by the *Mercury* on 23 March 1875:

For more than twenty years he has been a quiet, well-behaved man.... Yesterday he had allowed the demon drink to get the mastery of him, and having been incapable of taking care of himself, was conveyed to the lock-up. Even this is not Martin Cash's failing, and there is a tinge of romance mingled with regret at his yesterday's condition. It appears that some weeks ago Cash had a son, a young lad of 16 or 17 summers, the pride of his father's heart. The young lad sickened and died, and the bereaved parent has not been himself since. Perhaps some kind Samaritan may speak a comforting word to the old man, and help save him from himself.

The tone of the article conveyed the goodwill shown towards Cash until his death on 27 August 1877.

A particularly gruesome escape from the settlement occurred in September 1837, involving William Cripps (alias Major), who was serving a life sentence, and Abraham Reed. The two men bolted on 21 September, and a week later Cripps was captured, alone. With him he had a quantity of partly boiled, partly roasted meat, which he claimed was putrid; he wanted to dispose of it. According to Cripps's story, Reed had drowned while fishing at Curiosity Beach. 'The rascal gives so very vague an account of the Flesh that the suspicion already formed appears to strengthen', Booth wrote grimly in his journal on 29 September, the day after Cripps's capture.

The meat was examined and found not to be bad. Not only that, it was said to have human hairs adhering to it. Near Curiosity Beach there were some partially burnt bones in the ashes of a fire which Cripps said were the bones of a badger (wombat) he had killed. But the medical officer who examined the bones said that they were human bones. Although Cripps was charged with the murder of Reed, there was evidently not sufficient evidence, and he was tried for absconding and transported to Norfolk Island. There he probably died, for the authorities could find no trace of him in 1849.[6]

Makeshift craft of peculiar shapes and sizes were often manufactured by prisoners who imagined that their chances of escape were greater by sea than by way of Eaglehawk Neck. Occasionally, too, whaleboats were stolen from Port Arthur by groups of prisoners—for instance, eight men in 1839 and six in 1844—but it was more usual for men to make rough canoes or rafts after absconding and finding a secluded bay.

Occasionally, escapees were picked up by fishing boats that hovered near the coast, even though privately owned vessels were not permitted to approach within about 5 kilometres of Tasman Peninsula coastline. In the early 1860s, two prisoners escaped in this way and one of them eventually reached New South Wales, where he was recaptured. By the 1850s, small parties of constables were stationed along the coast to prevent escapes and canoe-building. Between 1855 and 1862, 205 escape attempts were made and of these, 187 men were recaptured and eighteen probably drowned, or died in the dense bush on the peninsula. Only one of the escapees had committed an offence in the colony during those years—horse-stealing—and he was captured and returned to Port Arthur. In 1872, not one prisoner out of 338 men attempted to escape.[7]

Some remarkable canoes and rafts were made by escapees. 'Captured a very neat Canoe from the Runaways', wrote Booth in his journal, after destroying several sheets of bark intended for another craft. He described one canoe as 'not fit for Ducks to swim in', a prisoner who was captured while floating away on an 'ingenious contraption' made of two barrels, and an 'extraordinary machine containing professional tools', seen drifting after its owner had probably drowned.

On the commandant's verandah in 1837, 'about a dozen most

V. R.

NOTICE !

COMPTROLLER-GENERAL'S OFFICE,
12th October, 1865.

FISHERMEN and OTHERS are hereby cautioned against visiting the Coasts of TASMAN'S or FORESTIER'S PENINSULAS, without the usual License from HIS EXCELLENCY THE GOVERNOR, as required by the Act of Council, 8th Vict., No. 14, Section 14. Any Person found without such License will be arrested and proceeded against according to Law. Fishermen who may have procured Licenses are reminded that such are only valid during the period for which they were granted.

W. NAIRN,

Comptroller-General.

A warning to fishermen and other boat owners. Occasionally, convicts were able to escape on fishing boats anchored in a secluded bay.

wretched attempts at boats and canoes' were lined up, craft fit only for men who attempted escape in desperation or madness, reported the *Hobart Town Almanack*. Other weird craft included 'a sort of packing case' and 'several coracles, the frame-work of wattle boughs, the covering (to serve for planking) of cotton shirts', described by David Burn. On one occasion an unsuccessful escapee claimed he had made his bark canoe in less than an hour, so Booth, apparently disbelieving, was said to have offered him a lesser punishment if he could prove his claim. He did so in fifty minutes, and on a trial run to the Isle of the Dead and back to the settlement, the canoe proved to be almost watertight. One of the most successful canoe-builders was said to be William Bickle, who absconded on three occasions, although he was recaptured each time. During his third attempt at freedom, he was picked up by the police while he was enjoying the Hobart Town Regatta.[8]

In 1839, Booth's confidence must have been shaken severely when eight men made an audacious escape in his six-oared whaleboat, and sailed away in the hope of freedom. As soon as the news reached Booth he gave chase for nearly five hours in a smaller, inferior whaleboat, until the escapees had sailed out of sight in their black, red and white craft. The hazy weather prevented a semaphore signal being sent to notify the authorities, so Booth, 'with no little mortification and regret', wrote a report to his superiors, in which he described how the escapees, six of them comprising the boat's regular crew, had taken the whaleboat from the slip in a cool and deliberate manner. As Booth had had word of the planned escape and ordered precautions that had not been carried out properly, his embarrassment was understandable.[9]   While ships searched for the whaleboat, the convicts navigated the dangerous seas off the colony's west coast, doubled back to the south past Capes Raoul and Pillar and continued along the east coast. On the way, they were courteous to the settlers they encountered in remote coastal areas, where they made peaceable raids for food, clothing, and firearms. In a report to the authorities in Hobart, one of the settlers wrote of the 'greatest Respect, civility and Attention' shown to him by the escapees, and at first sight their orderliness and neat dress, he explained, had almost convinced him that they were, as they claimed to be, from a government boat.

The escapees crossed Bass Strait, calling at Flinders Island, where one of the men decided to stay. They had planned to sail to New Zealand. But after three gruelling months in an open boat barely 5 metres long, by which time its sails must have been in tatters, their destination proved to be Twofold Bay on the New South Wales coast. There they were apprehended, taken to Sydney, and later tried in Hobart.[10]

One of the last 'escapes' from Port Arthur, and perhaps the saddest, could have been by land or by sea. It occurred during 1876–7 when the settlement was nearing its end. While a number of the mentally ill convicts were collecting firewood, probably for use in the asylum, a 61-year-old man in good physical health slipped away from the group. A search for him continued for several days, but the Commandant, Dr John Coverdale, reported that 'no trace whatever could be discovered of the unfortunate imbecile'.[11]

11   The Quick and the Dead

After transportation ended in 1853 and the colony achieved responsible government in 1856, there was 'an embarrassingly antagonistic feeling' between the British representative—the lieut.-governor—and the local government about the Convict Department, which was an 'Imperial' establishment. So the control of the department was transferred to the colony, and costs shared between the two governments, depending on whether a convict had been convicted in the colony or in Britain. Property also began to be transferred. By 1861, only Port Arthur, the Hobart penitentiary, and the Cascades Female Factory for convicts (later extended for invalids and the mentally ill) remained the financial responsibility of the British authorities. Finally, in 1871, Port Arthur's transfer took place.[1]

The antagonism continued, however, because the Tasmanian government asked for £5000 for the purpose of returning destitute ex-convicts to England, and the plan was sharply rejected. Nor was the Western Australian Governor, A. E. Kennedy, or his superiors in London, enthused by Tasmania's suggestion that after some Port Arthur men received their tickets-of-leave they should be removed to his colony. Reports he had read revealed them as 'incorrigible', not to mention in 'the most hopeless degree of degradation', and while Western Australia had accepted many convicts of the worst kind, he was not about to take Tasmania's dregs.[2]

By now Port Arthur's future was in jeopardy because the population of this extensive settlement—able to accommodate several thousand men in the old and new penitentiaries and the separate prison—was dwindling. Although many prisoners had been sentenced to life imprisonment to the settlement, none had ever been detained there for life, because after a period of up to ten years fixed by the lieut.-governor, they usually became eligible to return to the colony under a different classification, such as a ticket-of-leave. When transportation ended some men were still serving sentences there, and others would be admitted, including some colonial-born prisoners.[3] As well, between 1854 and 1856, Port Arthur received Norfolk Island men while the island settlement was being evacuated, including some who had already been at the Tasman Peninsula settlement. As had always been the case, the men continued to circulate—'each in his appropriate place'.

The settlement had always received a proportion of elderly convicts. Even as early as the 1830s, several were more than seventy years old—one was seventy-eight in 1837—and that year a medical board, after investigating eleven convicts, decided they deserved the comforts of a daily allowance of tea and sugar and a winter suit of woollen clothing.[4] As time passed, the numbers of elderly convicts increased, not only in the colony but at Port Arthur. For example in 1861, of 517 convicts at the settlement, two were between 70 and 80 years old and forty between 60 and 70.[5]

In the colony the infirm, the destitute, and the mentally ill were provided for, as well as the children of transportees, at institutions such as the Brickfields Invalid Depot for men, the Female Factory Nursery, the Van Diemen's Land Asylum for 'fallen' women, and the 'Lock' (the contagious diseases hospital). By 1848, the numbers of mentally ill patients had increased, so the New Norfolk Hospital was reorganized for the insane only, and invalid and aged ex-convicts were transferred to Impression Bay station on Tasman Peninsula. Twenty-six old men refused to leave New Norfolk, for what they imagined was a penal settlement, and wanted to die where they were. Finally, thirteen agreed to move and the remaining ten were ejected with as little violence as possible, even though they had no means of support.[6]

In 1857, the Impression Bay station was transferred to Port Arthur. Some pathetic, confused old men arrived, not understanding the reason for the move because they had not committed a crime. In 1861, there were 275 invalids and/or paupers at the settlement: four were aged between 90 and 100 years, eighteen between 80 and 90, fifty-six between 70 and 80. Their infirmities included blindness, paralysis, fits, chronic rheumatism, ruptures and senility.[7] At that time the authorities were concerned that the paupers were under regulations 'too nearly approaching those of a Penal Establishment', were cut off from society, and placed 'beyond the reach of such sympathy and kind attention' as charitable organizations might be able to offer.[8]

Some old men left Port Arthur as soon as possible, because they were free to do so, and would subsist by begging. One who left in February 1871 after only about eight days, and did not return, was 87-year-old James Cave. A veteran of the Peninsular War of 1808–14 in Spain, he had been transported for house-breaking and arrived in the colony in 1831. His wife, Eliza, and their three children probably remained in England.[9]

The old men were given free passages to and from the settlement by steamer and in March 1870, a *Mercury* reporter observed one of them who was returning, noting at the same time that he was one of those for whom the colony provided very comfortable quarters, amusement and food, and a free passage whenever they felt inclined to visit friends or have some recreation. He continued:

He was of low stature, very repulsive looking, dressed in an old sparrow-tail coat, that had no doubt at one time adorned a very genteel person, but which, under the present circumstances, appeared very much out of place. His head was covered with an old cloth cap, and his feet were *not* covered with a very dilapidated couple (not pairs) of shoes. He, too, had provided for himself, for under his arm was a bundle containing sundry scraps, the result very likely of the previous day's begging. This sketch will convey a very inadequate idea of this 'old gentleman', whose restlessness and imbecility were such as to give one an idea of a wild animal. . . .

In the 1860s, Mark Jeffrey made about eight visits to Port Arthur, as a destitute invalid. Despite his badly ulcerated leg, he managed to commit four assaults, possibly by lashing out with his two walking sticks, so he spent twenty-seven months in the separate prison and eighty days in solitary confinement. Finally, Jeffrey relinquished his pauper status in December 1871 and the reason was not pleasant. Jeffrey claimed that James Hunt had called him a flagellator, so he brutally assaulted him, saying that he would 'kill any b—— dog who called him by that name' because he had never been a flagellator. At the trial most of the witnesses were unreliable: the three women said they had been 'a little in drink', 'under the influence' and 'partly in liquor' and the male witness said he was 'that drunk he could not say what took place'. The jury returned the verdict of manslaughter and Jeffrey became a life prisoner at Port Arthur.[10]

Although the old penitentiary was so decrepit that it had been replaced in 1857 by the converted mill and granary, that year it became the home of the paupers and invalids, as well as the mentally ill for a time. The quarters were altered and greatly improved, but with a few years they were unsatisfactory and new dormitories were built.[11] The men were reasonably comfortable, had iron beds, mattresses, blankets and rugs, and fireplaces to warm their old bones.

They were given light duties, which amounted to occupa-

Mark Jeffrey, known as Big Mark, was at Port Arthur for many years, both as a prisoner and a destitute invalid. This photograph appeared in the first edition of his book, A Burglar's Life, *published in 1893 in Launceston and described as 'a Colonial Shilling Shocker' by one newspaper in Tasmania. Jeffrey had the unpleasant habit of lashing out with his walking-sticks, so in self-defence one government official used to arm himself with a heavy ebony ruler up his sleeve.*

tional therapy, such as acting as wardsmen to other old men, cooking, gathering firewood and regulating the clocks, for which they were paid sixpence to a shilling a day.[12] When Marcus Clarke visited Port Arthur in 1870, he noticed some of 'the jetsam' of transportation making a pretence of gardening. One man sat on the fountain, 'rubbing it tenderly with his hand'. Clarke was told that 'they've no home but this, and the commandant makes them do *something*'.[13]

At Christmas, the aged and the infirm enjoyed the festivities as much as the prisoners and the mentally ill: 'If these old gentlemen could neither dance nor sing, they could eat and drink well, and hobble about the Settlement with an inward, placid satisfaction', reported the *Mercury* in December 1860. There were, no doubt, a few who wandered too far if they were not too feeble, like the mentally ill man who disappeared one day in 1876 and was never seen again.

In 1874, when Port Arthur was nearing its end, all the paupers and invalids fit to travel were transferred to institutions in Hobart. Only two years later, in 1876, the pauper infirmary was reopened because the Cascades Invalid Depot was so overcrowded that men were sleeping on the floor and the Brickfields Invalid Depot totally lacked comfort for old men. A hundred men packed their scant belongings and feebly made their way to the steamer that would take them to Port Arthur.[14]

In 1857, mentally ill ex-convicts had also been transferred to the settlement to the old penitentiary, but they were soon moved to a military barracks, which was no longer required. At the time there were eighty-seven men: two were between 70 and 80 years of age, two between 60 and 70, five between 50 and 60 and seventy-eight were under 50 years.[15]

Occasionally some of the Port Arthur prisoners were temporarily removed to the asylum because the cells for the criminally insane in a wing of the separate prison were some-

The asylum as it is today, without the front wing and verandahs and with the tower turned front on. The skylight is at the top of the lofty ceiling of the dining-room, which has been faithfully restored. A wing to the left of the tower contains the museum.

The invalid and pauper infirmary or depot, at left, and the brick asylum (next to the separate prison). The latter was completed in 1867, and destroyed by fire in 1895, after which it was rebuilt by a local man, Harry Frerk. He turned the clock tower to its present angle.

times needed for prisoners. In James Boyd's opinion, these mentally ill convicts had 'impaired intellect', caused by the length of time they had been convicts and by their having 'little or no control over their evil propensities and irregular habits'.[16]

In 1872, by which time there was a new, brick asylum, ten of the 111 patients were Port Arthur convicts and the rest had been convicts, but not necessarily at the settlement. Of the total, three patients were in the asylum for the sixth time, one for the fourth time, six for the third time and nine for the second time. Two had been inmates of asylums for eighteen years, and eight were discharged as cured. At this time one man was 92 years old, ten were between 70 and 90, twenty-two between 60 and 70.[17]

By November 1867, the new asylum was near completion. Situated next to the separate prison and intended to provide for a hundred patients, the building was divided into twenty separate rooms with spacious amusement and recreation areas. In the centre was the dining-hall, with a lofty timber ceiling and columns, which has been restored. The main entrance, on each side of which were verandahs, was below a clock tower.[18]

At Port Arthur, the treatment of the mentally ill was typical of the times, but the doctors there lacked experience in asylums. During 1862, three canvas straight-jackets were made by convicts in the separate prison for use in the asylum. Also, convict carpenters constructed a shower-bath, which was probably a wooden box with a glass hole through which the patient could be observed during treatment with water—a punitive form of shock therapy.[19] (Water-baths were used as a punishment at prisons such as Sing Sing.)

In his annual report for 1872, the medical officer, Dr E. C. McCarthy, remarked that he felt very often the need for advice from the Commissioners of Hospitals for the Insane, who so far had not visited Port Arthur. In the asylum that year no restraint or punishment had been used, except seclusion in cells for some men, who were given exercise daily. There had been 64 cases of dementia, 40 of mania and 7 of melancholia among the 111 patients. They had received large doses of a sedative, bromide of potassium, and in his opinion it had improved the condition of some but none had been cured.[20]

In 1870, Marcus Clarke described the criminally insane as 'of but two dispositions—they cowered and crawled like whipped fox-hounds to the feet of their keepers, or they raged, howling blasphemous and hideous imprecations upon their gaolers'. He was eager to see a prisoner there, 51-year-old Edward Mooney, who had been described as the worst convict in the colony. Transported in the 1830s to New South Wales, Mooney was first sent to Port Arthur in 1850 from Norfolk Island. He received a ticket-of-leave in 1860, but in the same year he was convicted of assault and robbery and the death sentence was commuted to life imprisonment. He was frequently in the separate prison and was transferred to the asylum in 1868.

At Mooney's cell the warder uncovered a peep-hole in the barred door and Clarke peered through it and saw 'a grizzled, gaunt, and half-naked old man coiled in a corner'. Clarke wrote:

The gibbering animal within turned, and his malignant eyes met mine. 'Take care,' said the gaoler; 'he has a habit of sticking his finger through the peep-hole to try and poke someone's eyes out!' I drew back, and a nail-bitten hairy finger, like the toe of an ape, was thrust with rapid and simian neatness through the aperture. 'That is how he amuses himself,' said the good warder, forcing-to the iron slot; 'he'd best be dead, I'm thinking.'[21]

While there were some who presented an equally tragic appearance as Mooney, others were able to go on excursions, play draughts or dominoes, and listen to a violin and a harmonium that sometimes were played for them. Books were provided, although they were at times destroyed, and pen, ink, and paper were available for those who wished to write letters, as well as assistance to do so if they needed it.[22]

At Christmas, the mentally ill patients enjoyed plum pudding, as did the paupers and the prisoners, and they provided their own entertainment. For example, on Christmas Day in 1860, sets and a curtain were improvised, and the patients staged a three-act play. They also performed songs and recitations, and 'little nigger extravaganzas, comic and sentimental, with horn-pipes and jigs, sham quadrilles and waltzes, even polkas, marches, galoppes, and mazurkas, so far as music was concerned'. The patients continued their festivities 'until long past 8 o'clock with much spirit and good humor, evincing talent and very excellent mimicry that would have perplexed a Lunacy Commission or even a psychologist to pronounce them "cranky"'.[23]

During 1875, the chaplain, Rowland Haywood, remarked that the treatment of the mentally ill at Port Arthur was 'very kind and considerate'. Two years later, however, in February 1877, when the settlement was drawing to its close, a report in the *Mercury* contained some pertinent observations:

I know that opinions differ as to the proper treatment of lunatics, but I hardly think that the treatment of the Port Arthur lunatics would commend itself to anyone. I do not for a moment wish to be understood as implying that [they] are ill-treated. But it seems to me that the men are placed in the asylum not to be cured, but to be taken care of, and prevented from doing mischief. Criminal lunatics are better dead than alive, I dare say, still, so long as we do not make a practice of killing them outright, and so getting rid of them for good and all, some attempt should be made to bring back the absent reason. Not one man, I am credibly informed, has ever left the Port Arthur asylum perfectly cured. In the interests of common humanity, no lunatic asylum, and especially one so large as this at Port Arthur, should be left without a medical superintendent; but here, if an inmate behaves himself well he is tolerated; if he is noisy he is controlled; and if he dies there is an end of him.

Across the bay from Port Arthur is a small island—first named Opossum Island after Captain John Welsh's ship, which sailed into the harbour in 1827 to seek shelter. After the settlement's first chaplain, the Reverend John Manton (a Wesleyan missionary) arrived in 1832, he selected part of it as 'a secure and undisturbed resting-place' for the convicts who died at the settlement, and the name was changed to Isle de Mort, or the Isle of the Dead, as it is known today. To the convicts it was Little Island, or, more often, Dead Island.[24]

The earliest burial on the island was apparently that of 27-year-old Private Joseph Kerr of the 59th Regiment, whose simple headstone bears the date 13 May 1831. According to the inscription on the stone, the grave was moved to its present site where the free are buried, after Manton selected the site for the convict graves. By 1836, there were forty-three graves on the island.[25] Another early burial may have been an Aborigine's— an elderly woman who died during a voyage on the brig *Tamar* and was buried in a blanket at Port Arthur in August 1833. (Cremation was the usual Tasmanian Aboriginal means of disposing of the dead, but tree and ground burials also occurred.)[26] However, as the Aborigines who disembarked briefly at Port Arthur in the early 1830s were segregated from the settlement people—apart from those few who wanted to observe them—the old woman may have been segregated in death, as in life.

In the same year, 1833, Dennis Collins was buried on the island. He was a 58-year-old sailor with one leg who achieved notoriety in 1832 by hurling a stone at King William the Fourth at the Ascot races. The reason Collins gave for his action was that he had petitioned for the return of his pension and was refused. Collins was convicted of high treason and transported.[27] In *The Isle of the Dead*, Manton explains the circumstances of Collins's death:

[he] was required to do some light work, his age and general decrepitude, exempting him from the more severely worked gangs. Collins, however, declared his determination not to ... saying, that he had

No more pathetic relic exists of Port Arthur than this late nineteenth-century photograph of the graves of convicts on the Isle of the Dead. The view may date from before the settlement was closed in 1877, or after 1892, when a small government grant enabled the neglected graves and tombstones to be cleared of weeds. There were two sheds on the island—one for the grave-digger and the other to shelter funeral parties.

worked for the King long enough; and that he would neither perform the King's task, nor eat the King's food, any longer. He was sent to a cell, where he remained fourteen days, obstinately refusing either to eat or to work. He was reasoned with on the impropriety of his conduct, and urged to abandon his sinful resolution; but he exhibited a degree of steadfastness of purpose almost unparalleled. At the end of the period ... he was taken to the hospital, where every medical comfort which that establishment afforded was set before him; but all was insufficient to overcome his resolution; he lingered for seven days longer ....

Nothing marks the grave of Collins, who died on 1 November 1833. Manton remarked that sometimes the surviving prisoners would have liked to erect a gravestone as 'an act of kindness' after a burial.

In the 1860s, among the trees on the island, geraniums and other flowers were planted by the convict John Barron. He had been transported from Limerick in Ireland in 1850 for receiving stolen goods and arrived in the colony in 1853. In 1856, he was convicted of a serious offence, and instead of being hanged, he was sent to Port Arthur.[28] Anthony Trollope, who met him in 1872, described him as quiet, unobtrusive and moody. He preferred digging graves to life at the settlement, and always had two prepared—one for a Catholic and one for a Protestant. (He was acting against orders.) After some years on the Isle of the Dead he was unhappy and wanted to work his passage to America to begin a new life, although he was sixty years old.

By the mid 1870s, having driven the staff to distraction, Mark Jeffrey became the grave-digger. According to *A Burglar's Life*, he asked in 1875 if he could take charge of the island, although the Commandant, Dr Coverdale, recommended his removal there 'where he can be safely and separately kept'. Permission was granted, providing that Jeffrey was prevented from assaulting visitors to the island. The convict was rowed there on Monday mornings and returned on Saturday afternoons to the settlement. As had Barron, he lived in a hut and he also baked his own 'first-class bread'. On the island, Jeffrey proved to be as much of a nuisance as he was at the settlement: to attract the attention of the staff he would light a fire, but when someone rowed over in response to the signal, all he would want was a box of matches.[29]

Eventually, Jeffrey was returned to the settlement and ultimately to the separate prison, where he was as obstreperous as ever. During a visit to Port Arthur, the attorney-general suggested that Jeffrey might be removed to the Isle of the Dead again. In a copy of a letter Jeffrey wrote on slate to Dr Coverdale, he employed his usual attempt at 'official' correspondence, which he thought was the correct form, after having heard constables in court giving evidence in a similar way.[30]

The Turn. A. General asked me Jeffrey if I Jeffrey would go back to Dead Island if he got the chimney done [there] and I Jeffrey then told the Turner General that I Jeffrey would rather not. And now if you ... will be pleased to see me Jeffrey, I Jeffrey will tell you ... what conditions I Jeffrey would go back ... and on these conditions you ... can send me Jeffrey back to Dead Island whenever you please.[31]

Coverdale had a sound understanding of Jeffrey, as had other officials such as Governor Frederick Weld, who in 1877 wrote to the commandant that 'Mark Jeffrey, it must be remembered, has suffered much ... what I see in Jeffrey's letters is a mind unhinged by crime and suffering.... He knows too truly that if irritated he may again commit himself and he trusts that authority will help him to control himself.... Ought authority to refuse? I say No.'[32]

Some 1700 convicts in unmarked graves—and perhaps some paupers and mentally ill men—are buried on the Isle of the Dead, as well as about 180 free people—military and civil staff and their families. Seventy-six headstones for the latter remain and are being restored. But the metal numbers that marked each convict grave had long since disappeared in the 1920s, when an elderly guide, Alfred Mawle (whose father had been employed at the settlement) described them to George Porter, author of *Wanderings in Tasmania*.

In the later years of the settlement's history, convict funerals became less crude. In 1840, according to the Canadian convict, Linus Miller, who assisted with burials for a time while he was the church clerk, the bodies were first dissected and then placed without shrouds in a rough coffin. Four men carried the coffin to the wharf and rowed it across to the island. By the 1860s,

Some of the graves of the free people—military and civil staff and their families—photographed in the nineteenth century. The vaults and gravestones are being restored.

some of the graves of the Catholic prisoners had 'a rude wooden cross at the head, and in one or two instances, a board contained the names'.[33]

One of the last funerals to take place was attended by a visitor, who described it in the *Clipper* in July 1893. The convict had been in the hospital, and when his death was near, his wife was sent for from Glenorchy near Hobart, but she arrived too late:

The body was conveyed from the hospital to the church ... the bell being tolled at intervals meanwhile. Here the usual portion of the burial service took place, after which the coffin was conveyed down the oak avenue ... where two boats were in waiting, one manned by a crew all dressed in white, the other empty. On the latter the coffin was lowered ... and [it] was taken in tow ... a procession was formed which was conducted by the grave-digger over and among the graves....[34]

Soon a tangle of weeds and bracken grew about the graves and Barron's garden, and in 1892 a small government grant enabled the shockingly neglected condition of the Isle of the Dead to be improved because it was a disgrace to the town and visitors might 'blush that civilisation could tolerate such a sacred historical spot to be overrun with scrub'. By 1910, however, Archibald Marshall would note in *Sunny Australia* how he 'stepped over the graves of the prisoners, for there was nothing to show where they were'. Meanwhile, at the settlement, the living—perhaps better described as living dead—were merely existing in the pauper infirmary and the asylum. Some of the mentally ill were anxious to know why they were there against their will now that 'their time was up', apparently believing that they had been sentenced to Port Arthur.[35]

12   The Curtain Falls

In the 1870s, a Select Committee found that proper penal discipline was impossible to carry out at Port Arthur and the settlement's cost was excessive for the small numbers of men accommodated there. It was to be closed as soon as possible, but it remained open until 1877, inadequately staffed. Within a few years, in 1873, nearly all the buildings were so dilapidated that rain was causing damage to ceilings, walls, and floors, and the cost of repairs was estimated at £4000. Among the repairs needed were new shingles on nearly every building, including the penitentiary, the church and the separate prison. As well, the church spire was beginning to fall apart, some of its stonework was in poor condition, and the canvas awning over the verandah of Government Cottage required replacing.[1]

According to the *Mercury* in January 1874, the 'breaking up of Port Arthur is proceeding more rapidly than the public have any idea of'. The settlement was breaking up in more ways than one, but the newspaper was referring to the transfer of some men to Hobart. In January 1877, the population of Port Arthur was 64 prisoners, 126 paupers and 79 mentally ill patients, and in March that year the government finally took steps towards removing all the men.

First, more space had to be made available at the Cascades Invalid Depot for the aged and chronically ill, where, in 1871, it had been 'a positive cruelty' to use this gloomy old prison as

A John Watt Beattie photograph, captioned 'a well-known Port Arthur identity'. He was probably one of the old ex-convicts who lived at the settlement after it closed.

their refuge. The depot for females and males had been opened in 1869 in part of the Cascades Female Factory, and now the female invalids had to be transferred elsewhere.[2]

In March 1877, Coverdale notified his superiors that twenty paupers had left Port Arthur aboard the *Harriet*, and from the wharf at Hobart they were conveyed in a van to the Cascades Depot. In mid April, an inspector of police and a number of constables went to Port Arthur on the *Southern Cross* to help escort the remaining forty-seven prisoners—and twenty-three aged paupers—to town, and the steamer returned to collect eighty mentally ill men, eight of whom were under sentence.[3]

On those April days, when prisoners (handcuffed and in leg-irons), paupers and the mentally ill arrived at the wharves in Hobart, large inquisitive crowds gathered and had to be moved on by the police. The old paupers were helped into carts, well-padded with straw for their comfort, and the mentally ill into a similar vehicle. And the prisoners, including Mark Jeffrey, Daniel Ahern, Thomas Meaghan, William Yeomans and Allan Williamson, were marched ashore and stowed in carts with benches. As the prisoners' carts moved off to the Campbell Street gaol, the town's loafers followed. One of the last prisoners, 50-year-old Luke Marshall, was taken to hospital with a fractured spine. Near Port Arthur he had jumped aboard a tram-waggon (probably carrying firewood) but when the speed down a steep descent increased, he became frightened and jumped off.[4]

Meanwhile, the staff at the settlement had prepared to leave, making packing cases from some of the boards of the graceful old church spire, which had been blown down in a storm in about 1875. The government had not considered the spire worth repairing, and according to Coverdale, the boards were 'worth little more than to make crates or packing cases' because of their various lengths, nail holes and the sanding on one side to represent stone.[5]

Dr Coverdale, a few staff and seven well-behaved, able-bodied prisoners remained at the settlement until September 1877 to dismantle it. The fittings in the penitentiary, separate prison, hospital, invalid depot and asylum were left untouched, only the furniture being forwarded to town, and the church, its furniture and fittings were left as they were. Both the penitentiary turret clock and the church clock were removed.[6]

Finally, in September 1877, the doors of the buildings were locked, and the settlement was left in the charge of a caretaker, John Evenden. Another resident of long-standing, Joseph Mawle, who had had various positions at the settlement, decided to occupy one of the houses with his family. And a pauper, having become accustomed to his 'home' there, was allowed to stay on 'at his urgent request', probably to become one of the Port Arthur guides of the late nineteenth century.[7]

In 1878, Dr Coverdale became the surgeon superintendent of the Cascades Hospital for the Insane. At this time, the pauper invalids were still in one of the old buildings, which had been lime-washed, painted and generally improved for them as much as was possible. When the aged invalids moved in, they had been described as 'much neglected' and the other elderly men 'quite incapacitated' from looking after 'the unfortunate old men placed under their care' at Port Arthur. The description of their condition did not spare the feelings of Coverdale.[8]

The mentally ill remained at this institution until 1890, when the criminally insane were moved to the Hobart gaol for three years. In the early 1890s, any of the original group who were

The commandant from 1874 to 1877, Dr John Coverdale, was known to the men as 'Black Jack'. Before moving to the settlement, he was the superintendent of the Queen's Orphan School. When Coverdale died in 1896 at the age of seventy-two, he was the oldest medical practitioner in the colony.

still alive were to become patients at the New Norfolk Asylum (now the Royal Derwent Hospital). As for the paupers, in 1879 they were transferred again to the New Town Charitable Institution (formerly the Queen's Orphan School and now St John's Park Hospital).

A superb nineteenth-century view, taken before 1895 when the two-storey parsonage, at far left, was partly destroyed by fire. The photographer, T. C. Crawford, shows the rear of the guard tower at right, the rear of the penitentiary, the church, and Government Cottage, with smoke coming from its chimney.

13   A New Act

To the *Tasmanian Mail*, in September 1877, Port Arthur was wiped from the map and with its closing 'passed away the last stain which remained upon Tasmania'. In that year the settlement became known officially as Carnarvon, probably after the Colonial Secretary, Lord ('Twitters') Carnarvon, by people who wished to obliterate all traces of the hated stain.[1] Soon the names of other places on Tasman Peninsula with convict backgrounds were also changed: Wedge Bay convict station became Nubeena, the Cascades became Koonya and the Norfolk Bay station became Taranna. Inevitably, as more and more tourist publications began to describe the attractions of Port Arthur both names were used in them, but the name Port Arthur was preferred by some Tasmanians who envisaged the tourist potential of the convict ruins.

Port Arthur grew slowly into a small town after the first sale of Crown Land took place on 28 December 1877. Colonists displayed little interest in the auction, perhaps because memories of that place of misery were too recent. But, in 1882, *Walch's Almanac* listed not only a post office at Port Arthur but a deputy registrar of births and, by 1886, a cricket club and a

---

William Thompson, a shoemaker, was transported for life for shopbreaking in 1841. In the same year he began serving two years' hard labour in chains at Port Arthur for absconding and larceny. In 1850, his punishment for looking at Miss Mary Ann Martin in a water-closet was six months' hard labour. Thompson received a conditional pardon in the early 1850s. He may have been dressed up in this garb by photographer Beattie, or he may have been the Thompson who was living rent free at Port Arthur in 1881. (There were six Thompsons or Thomsons at the settlement in 1861.)

lawn tennis club were thriving, Mrs E. Trenham was the teacher at the State school and Miss J. Blackwood was the post mistress. (The Carnarvon postmark was still used in the 1920s.) In July 1889, Carnarvon was proclaimed a town under the Town Boards Act, 1884.[2]

Among the earliest residents were a few men who split palings in the nearby bush for Henry Chesterman of Hobart. A man named Thompson, possibly the ex-convict, William Thompson, occupied a cottage there, rent free for a time, as did a number of others.[3] In 1880, when the population was about eighty, a visitor, James Edge Partington, was quite at a loss how to class the residents because they had no hotel and the fine church had not been used since Port Arthur was abandoned as a penal settlement. Partington had sallied forth to embark on the *Southern Cross* for Port Arthur, only to postpone his first attempt at going there because 800 people had the same idea. At the settlement, his guide, a former convict, told him some wonderful tales of convict life 'which from constant repetition he no doubt firmly believes'.[4]

On holidays and weekends, trippers often surged into Port Arthur by steamer, to the dismay of the caretaker, Evenden. On one occasion, although the visitors did no damage to government property, they trampled garden beds, raided fruit trees and insulted the residents.[5] The town lacked accommodation for tourists, as the *Australasian Sketcher* observed snootily in April 1884: 'Hobart people are slow in these matters, and unless it is taken in hand by Victorian and Sydney capitalists, there is not much hope.' In 1892, however, the *Handbook of Tasmania*

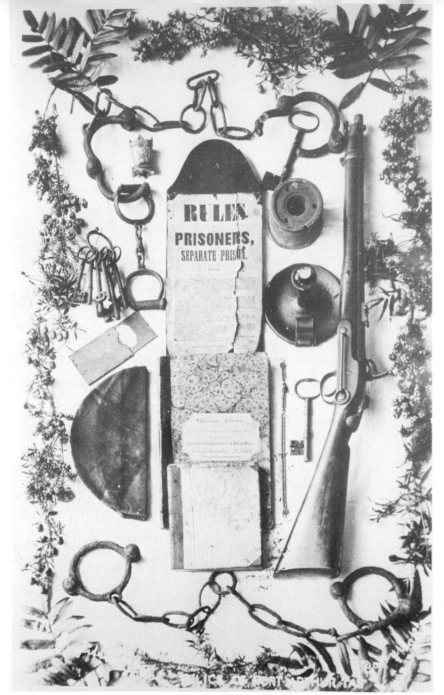

One of Beattie's many postcards relating to Port Arthur.

described not only a good hotel in the former commandant's residence, but a boarding-house as well. That year about 200 people lived in and around Port Arthur, and the *Handbook* noted that 'the tone of its society is refined and intellectual'. Obviously, the tourist authorities still felt the need to reassure its readers as to the town's respectability.

Although by 1881 some buildings had deteriorated further, the town remained basically the same as it had been as a penal settlement—until 1884. In March that year, the first major change came when sparks from a bushfire ignited the dry shingle roof of the lovely old church. From all directions residents rushed to the church with buckets and tubs of water, but the building burned to the ground. Only the bare walls were left, and until about 1890, or perhaps later, the spiral staircase in the tower.[6] The avenue of English trees leading to the church remained as a shady approach to the ruin, but eight years later, the fine stone columns at the entrance to the avenue became 'very much out of the perpendicular' on 27 January 1892.

One of the residents reported the incident to the *Tasmanian Mail* in February:

the inhabitants of this port were much alarmed by a violent shock of earthquake. It began by a low rumbling about 2.45 a.m., followed by a slight shock, the rumbling increasing in intensity for something like 10 or 12 seconds, when the second and heaviest shock occurred. There was a third but very slight shock.... The tall houses in this port vibrated and shook in an alarming manner, and many of the inmates rushed out on their verandahs in fear. A large brick wall at [the parsonage] is badly damaged and ready to fall.

At the next meeting of the Town Board a petition was received from residents and ratepayers requesting permission to remove the columns from the avenue to the public cemetery to improve its entrance.

In the early 1880s, when Evenden was still the caretaker, he

PORT ARTHUR

CARNARVON HOTEL, CARNARVON,

**Personally Patronised by their Excellencies
the Governor and the Admiral of the Fleet.**

OVERLAND Route.   SEA Route.

Particulars from Tourist Association, Lord.
Buildings, or JAMES LORIMER, Lessee.

An 1895 advertisement for the Carnarvon Hotel (the commandant's house). Port Arthur became known as Carnarvon in 1877.

Lithend, the second oldest residence at Port Arthur, during restoration in 1981.

The stone columns topped by urns, at the entrance to the church avenue, photographed in the late nineteenth century. In 1892, the columns—or one—were described as 'very much out of the perpendicular' after an earthquake. There is now a spherical stone on the top of each—probably the stones that were originally on either side of the steps to the commandant's house.

complained of uncleared, thick bush near the settlement. His concern was justified, because on 28 January 1895, a bush fire swept in. Near the church the former parsonage was partly destroyed and the neighbouring house on the corner narrowly missed, and Government Cottage—described in a newspaper report as 'a valuable relic of the past'—was ruined.

The fire roared about the town, attacking the old asylum, which had become Carnarvon Town Hall. The gymnasium in the hall was engulfed by flames that destroyed the athletic club's property, but residents managed to save the hall's piano. Next to the hall, the separate prison was too close to escape the flames, and it was gutted. On the hill above the town, the old military barracks was destroyed, and nearby, the hospital, purchased by Archbishop Daniel Murphy to convert into a college, was damaged. Those buildings that escaped damage included the Carnarvon Hotel, Trenville's Private Family Hotel (not far from the hospital), and the massive penitentiary.[7]

In the summer of 1897–8, bush fires were causing destruction, all around the colony. Money flowed in to help the homeless, and the singer Amy Sherwin, the 'Tasmanian Nightingale', held charity concerts. In January 1898, the *Mercury* reported that fate seemed determined that Port Arthur should be wiped out, because when fire swept Tasman Peninsula from end to end, in late December 1897, much of the town was a smouldering ruin.

The first building to catch alight was the four-storey penitentiary, which burned for forty-eight hours after the fire reached the town on 31 December.

There are many who will make no concealment of their satisfaction at the destruction of the Penitentiary. On holiday visits to Port Arthur in years gone by you always met the man who 'would like to put a limited quantity of dynamite or gunpowder' under the Model and the Penitentiary, and so remove the last trace of the 'system' that flourished there. . . .

While the fire was at its worst, some townspeople sheltered on the ketch *Mary*, which traded between Hobart and Port Arthur and had been anchored in the bay when the fire began. Most of them were homeless and they shook their heads and said 'the place is "gone"'. One old man, 75-year-old Henry Trenham, died in his home. Archbishop Murphy's hospital, which had been restored after the last fire, was beyond repair, but the town hall was intact, after having been rebuilt by a local man, Harry Frerk. It was similar to the original building although the clock tower was turned to a different angle.[8]

Within days after the fire, trippers were again arriving to inspect the fire-gutted buildings, wander through the ivy-covered church ruin, in which daisies were flourishing, and take boat trips to the Isle of the Dead. For about a shilling, guides, including Alfred Mawle, described the buildings and escorted visitors among the 'h'oaks, h'elms, and h'ashes' that had thrived for so long.

According to Charles Barrett in *Isle of Mountains*, Mawle was 'a delightful old fellow, with a repertoire of quaint sayings and a quaint way of imparting his knowledge'. Once he had begun his patter, 'standing heels together and feet placed in the correct quarter-to-four o'clock position', nothing could stop him and his 'pocket histories' were word perfect. He remained a guide until he was an elderly man.

Eventually, motor vehicles replaced coaches drawn by two or three horses. In the early twentieth century, Wellard's coach business was kept busy and Athol ('Snakey') Wellard, born in 1900 at the parsonage at Port Arthur, helped drive the coaches. In 1980, he recalled how his nickname originated: 'There was a part-Arab mare in the lead and I gave a hissing noise and she'd give me every mortal thing she had!' Mr Wellard, whose memories span seventy years or so, remembered well an ex-convict with the marks of lashes on his back, and recalled a guide who would whip off his shirt and startle visitors with his

A postcard of three Port Arthur guides, photographed probably in the early 1920s, are, from left, Alfred Mawle, Tom Free and Harry Frerk. Mr Frerk was responsible for the rebuilding of the town hall.

Scenes like these in the penitentiary, top, and the separate prison, bottom, were common at Port Arthur between 1877, when the settlement closed, and the 1890s. The view in the prison is of a wing opposite the chapel stairs, which have been restored, but the row of cells is badly damaged. The other two cell wings are restored.

'stripes'. When *For the Term of His Natural Life* was filmed on location at Port Arthur in the mid 1920s, Mr Wellard was among the many local people who had small parts in the film.

For many years Tasman Peninsula was isolated, and boats—some like 'a bloomin' grocer shop', according to Harold Clark of Nubeena, in his nineties—obtained provisions from them. In the late 1920s, however, Port Arthur residents and those nearby shopped at a general store built next to the penitentiary by William Radcliffe. He and his wife, Dora, began the shop with 'a little divvy' from Tattersall's Lottery. During the building, Radcliffe found relics of convict days on the site and these he hung on the walls of the store to begin the nucleus of a museum that grew famous among tourists. For many years,

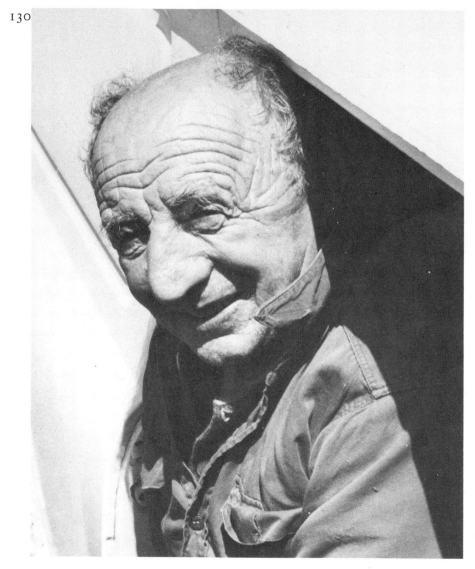

until 1974, when the contents of the museum were sold to the Tasmanian government, William Radcliffe's daughter, Lorna Smith, who lives on the outskirts of the settlement, kept the museum intact. Mrs Smith recalls that when she was a child 'nobody ever admitted to convict ancestry', but in the past few decades this attitude has slowly changed. In contrast, in the 1880s, Nisbet Hume wrote in *A Colonial Tramp*:

I got a warning from a friend who met me in Hobart that it was not 'good form' while in Tasmania to say anything about transportation, as one never knew whose feelings he might be wounding by alluding to the subject, so I took great care to be always on my guard.

As early as 1842, Port Arthur's future as a 'watering-place' for visitors was foreseen by David Burn, and later a former governor, Sir Charles du Cane, expressed similar, if grander, notions in his *Tasmania—Past and Present*:

If it were but in England, I could fancy an enterprising Hotel Company at once pouncing upon the Settlement and converting the huge Penitentiary into a vast Hotel, with all modern appliances and comforts. I could fancy railway trains and daily steamers bringing crowds of excursionists. I could fancy the shores of the Harbour covered with lodging-houses and bathing machines, and the Harbour itself dotted with yachts and pleasure boats.

Steamer excursions began not long after Sir Charles's book was published in 1877. During the Second World War the excellent harbour enabled the *Queen Mary* to anchor there, and today Russian cruise ships, as well as P. and O. liners, occasionally call. Coach trips have replaced the excursions by steamer from Hobart to Port Arthur, the *O'Hara Booth* busily plies between the settlement and the Isle of the Dead, and dotted around the bay at times are up to fifteen fishing boats which sail around the shores of Tasman Peninsula.

Mr Athol Wellard, born at Port Arthur in the parsonage in 1900, who drove horse-drawn tourist coaches in the early twentieth century.

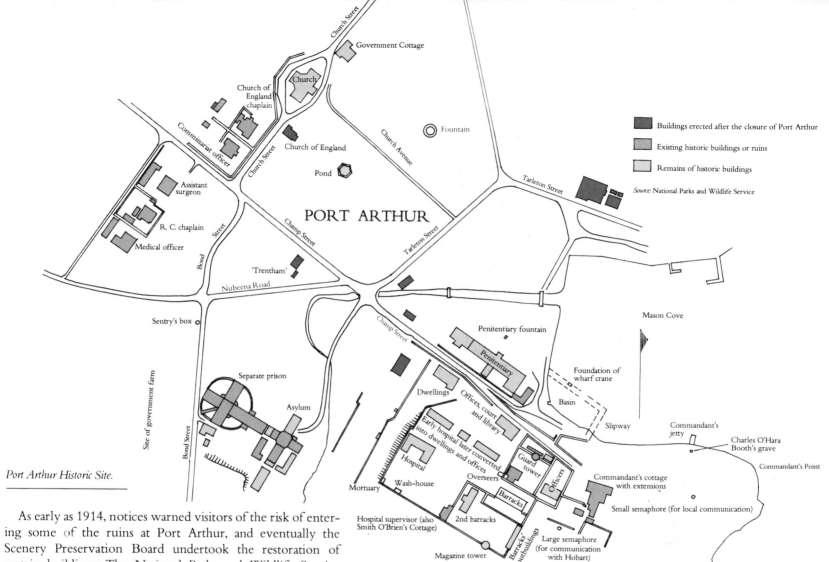

Port Arthur Historic Site.

As early as 1914, notices warned visitors of the risk of entering some of the ruins at Port Arthur, and eventually the Scenery Preservation Board undertook the restoration of certain buildings. The National Parks and Wildlife Service continues the formidable task of preserving and restoring Port Arthur Historic Site, which covers about 100 hectares and contains some sixty buildings.

Epilogue

Leonard Hand died at the age of twenty-five in 1876 at the Hobart gaol.

James Cave, who died at the age of ninety-five in August 1879 at the Brickfields Invalid Depot at Hobart, had the distinction of an obituary in the *Tasmanian Mail*. His 'general quiet manner, obliging disposition, and kind friendship' had endeared him to his fellow-inmates.

Thomas Meaghan was discharged from Hobart gaol in 1885.

In 1880, Edward 'Blind' Mooney lay in a helpless condition at the Cascades Hospital for the Insane, and died at the age of sixty-five in 1886.

In 1880 Daniel Ahern was seen wandering bare-footed 'like a wild beast' at the Cascades Hospital and he died at the age of sixty-three in 1887.

At the New Town Charitable Institution, where 'the poor people' were kept 'scrupulously clean', and it was well worth a visit for tourists, William Yeomans, a bachelor, died in about 1885. As late as 1898, 52 per cent of the men in this institution were ex-transportees.

Mark Jeffrey became a familiar figure in Launceston where he limped about the streets as a pedlar. He lived at the Launceston Invalid Depot, where he died in about 1903, possibly during a serious outbreak of smallpox in the city.

Notes

Abbreviations

BPP   British Parliamentary Papers (House of Commons
Papers Relating to Convict Discipline and
Transportation, unless otherwise stated)

CO   Colonial Office

CON   Convict Department

CSO   Colonial Secretary's Office

GO   Governor's Office

HL   House of Lords

THAJ   Tasmanian House of Assembly Journals

T.Leg.Co.J. Tasmanian Legislative Council Journals

SC   Select Committee on Transportation 1837

CSD   Colonial Secretary's Department

Introduction

1 John West, *The History of Tasmania*, p. 14.
2 Quoted in H. Reynolds. ' "That Hated Stain": The Aftermath of
Transportation in Tasmania', pp. 19–23:
3 *BBP*, vol. 42, 1843, p. 28.
4 E. N. C. Braddon, 'A Home in the Colonies', quoted in Reynolds,
op. cit., p. 27.
5 [Port Arthur Papers], *THAJ*, paper 100, 1863, p. 14.
6 Prison Discipline Report, 1867; *THAJ*, vol. 22, 1871.
7 *Mercury*, 7 October 1869.
8 *Tasmanian Mail*, 22 December 1877.

Chapter 1   An Important Public Benefit

1 *Hobart Town Courier*, 17 November 1827.
2 CSO1/217/5215.
3 John West, *The History of Tasmania*, p. 293.
4 CSO1/483/10748 and CSO1/3/30.
5 *Tasmanian & Austral-Asiatic Review*, 10 and 17 September 1830.
6 West, op. cit., p. 395.

7 CO280/247/28.
8 CSO1/483/10748.
9 ibid.
10 CSO1/484/10750.
11 CSO1/483/10748.
12 ibid.
13 John Frost, *The Horrors of Convict Life*, pp. 31–2.
14 CSO1/477/10639 and CSO1/484/10751.
15 CSO1/484/10750.
16 CSO1/477/10639.
17 CSO1/483/10748.
18 ibid.
19 ibid.
20 CSO1/477/10639.
21 CSO1/483/10748.
22 *BPP*, SC Evidence, vol. 22, 1838, p. 51; CSO1/498/10934 and
CSO1/551/12027.
23 CSO1/807/17244.
24 CSO1/551/12027.
25 CSO1/484/10750.
26 CSO1/498/10934.
27 CSO1/559/12337.
28 CO280/293/714–15.
29 T. J. Lempriere, *The Penal Settlements of Van Diemen's Land*, pp. 68–9.

Chapter 2   A Place for Everybody . . .

1 *BPP*, SC Appendix, vol. 19, 1837, p. 46.
2 ibid, p. 48.
3 CSO1/632/14299.
4 ibid.
5 N. J. B. Plomley (ed.), *Friendly Mission*, pp. 779 and 914.
6 *BPP*, vol. 19, op. cit., pp. 46 and 58.
7 ibid., pp. 58 and 52.
8 ibid., p. 56.

9 ibid., pp. 58–60.
10 ibid., p. 46.
11 CSO1/180/4324.
12 CSO1/566/12637.
13 A. G. L. Shaw, *Convicts & the Colonies*, pp. 148–51.
14 L. L. Robson, *The Convict Settlers of Australia*, pp. 143–4 and 146.
15 CON 31/45.
16 *Mercury*, 5 October and 2 November 1857.
17 CON 31/34 and *Tas. Leg. Co. J.*, vol. 26. 1878.
18 *BPP*, vol. 19, op. cit., p. 355.
19 CO714/149/1048.

Chapter 3   Absolute Powers

1 *Australian Dictionary of Biography*, vol. 1, p. 125; C. O. Booth, Journal, August 1832 and February 1833.
2 N. J. B. Plomley (ed.), *Friendly Mission*, p. 707.
3 Booth, op. cit., March 1833.
4 ibid.
5 1837 *Hobart Town Almanack*, p. 101.
6 CO280/258–9/48.
7 John West, *The History of Tasmania*, p. 448.
8 *BPP*, SC Appendix, vol. 19, 1837, pp. 51–2.
9 Booth, op. cit., October 1833.
10 James Backhouse and Charles Tylor (eds), *The Life and Labours of George Washington Walker*, p. 169.
11 James Backhouse, *A Narrative of a Visit to the Australian Colonies*, p. 168.
12 Backhouse and Tylor, op. cit.
13 Booth, op. cit., April 1834.
14 CO280/258–9/48.
15 CSO1/807/17244.
16 ibid.
17 *BPP*, HL, 1837, vol. 8, p. 113.
18 CSO1/635/14379.
19 ibid.; CSO1/807/17244; Booth, op. cit., December 1833.
20 1837 *Hobart Town Almanack*, op. cit., p. 102.
21 T. J. Lempriere, *The Penal Settlements of Van Diemen's Land*, pp. 73–5.
22 George Mackaness (ed.), *Some Private Correspondence of Sir John and Lady Jane Franklin*, part 1, pp. 33–4.
23 Lempriere, op. cit.; G. T. W. B. Boyes, 'Extracts from the Journal'.
24 Booth, op. cit., May 1838.
25 Mackaness, op. cit., p. 34.
26 Alexander Clark Letterbook.
27 *Australian Dictionary of Biography*, op. cit.
28 RS31/15 (4a), University of Tasmania Archives.

Chapter 4   Growth and Expansion

1 T. J. Lempriere, *The Penal Settlements of Van Diemen's Land*, pp. 106–07; 1837 *Hobart Town Almanack*, p. 92; Lempriere, op. cit., p. 111.
2 C. O. Booth, Instructions for Semaphore; W. E. Masters, *The Semaphore Telegraph System of Van Diemen's Land*, p. 29.
3 David Burn, 'Excursion to Port Arthur', p. 271.
4 *Australian Dictionary of Biography*, vol. 2, p. 71.
5 *St John the Baptist Magazine*, 1890, quoted in G. E. Robertson, *Early Buildings of Southern Tasmania*, vol. 2, p. 376.
6 Lempriere, op. cit., p. 86.
7 Booth, Journal, April 1836; Lempriere, op. cit., p. 111; Anthony Trollope, *Australia*, p. 509; H. Phibbs Fry, *A System of Penal Discipline*, p. 172.
8 H. Butler Stoney, *A Year in Tasmania*, p. 52; G. C. Mundy, *Our Antipodes*, p. 228.
9 CSO1/504/13194.
10 ibid.
11 CO280/258–9/48.
12 Letters of Col. George Arthur, 1825–36.
13 Lempriere, op. cit., pp. 109–10.
14 ibid., p. 110; Phibbs Fry, op. cit., p. 172; *BPP*, HL, vol. 11, 1847–8, p. 68.
15 Burn, op. cit., p. 268.
16 Lempriere, op. cit., p. 67; George Mackaness (ed.), *Some Private Correspondence of Sir John and Lady Jane Franklin*, part 1, pp. 14–16.
17 Butler Stoney, op. cit., p. 50.
18 G. W. T. B. Boyes, Diary, 1843.
19 CSO5/129/3067.
20 Clark Letterbook.
21 ibid.; *BPP*, vol. 11, op. cit., p. 68; *BPP*, vol. 48, 1847, pp. 138–9.
22 *BPP*, HL, vol. 11, 1851.

Chapter 5   Our Penal Settlement

1 Arthur Griffiths, *Secrets of the Prison-House*, vol. 1, p. 72.
2 *Tas. Leg. Co. J.*, vol. 6, 1861–2.

3 *BPP*, vol. 29, 1846, p. 30.
4 *BPP*, vol. 43, 1849, p. 148.
5 *BPP*, ibid., p. 41.
6 *BPP*, vol. 48, 1846, pp. 138–9; ibid., vol. 17, 1841, p. 137.
7 *BPP*, vol. 45, 1862, p. 93.
8 David Burn, 'Excursion to Port Arthur', pp. 274–5; *Australian Dictionary of Biography*, vol. 2, pp. 419–20.
9 *Australian Dictionary of Biography*, vol. 2, p. 293; John Evenden, Experiences of an Officer in the Convict Department, p. 64.
10 *BPP*, vol. 45, op. cit., p. 87.
11 *BPP*, vol. 17, op. cit., p. 126; vol. 43, op. cit., p. 181; *Tas. Leg. Co. J.*, vol. 9, 1863, p. 11; [Port Arthur Papers], *THAJ*, paper 3, 1872, p. 7.
12 *BPP*, vol. 14, 1857, p. 168.
13 CSO1/807/17244.
14 *THAJ*, vol. 22, 1871, pp. 12 and 16; *Mercury*, 7 October 1859, 24 March 1870, 18 February 1877.
15 *THAJ*, vol. 22, op. cit., p. 16.
16 CSO1/843/10748.
17 CSO22/90/1916.
18 *BPP*, HL, vol. 11, 1849, p. 37.
19 ibid., p. 39.
20 *Australian Dictionary of Biography*, vol. 3, p. 379; Henry White, *Crime and Criminals*, p. 147.
21 *BPP*, HL, vol. 11, op. cit., pp. 40–1.

Chapter 6   Our Town

1 *BPP*, vol. 29, 1846, p. 29.
2 Robert Crooke, *The Convict*, p. 113.
3 Dr Thomas Brownell, Diary.
4 Quoted in K. R. von Stieglitz (ed.), *Edward Markham's Van Diemen's Land Journal*.
5 *BPP*, HL, vol. 11, 1849, p. 41.
6 *Mercury*, 27 February 1839.
7 *Hobart Town Courier*, 8 March 1839.
8 David Burn, 'Excursion to Port Arthur', p. 286.
9 J. N. Propsting, Personal Recollections of Five Years at Port Arthur.
10 Tim Bobbin, *Revelations of P[ort] A[rthur]*.
11 Propsting, op. cit.
12 ibid.
13 *Mercury*, 10 August 1866.
14 F. Holdsworth, Colonel William Thomas Napier Champ.

15 H. Butler Stoney, *A Year in Tasmania*, p. 54.
16 Henry Melville, *The Present State of Australia*, p. 181.
17 Frederick Mackie, *Traveller Under Concern*, p. 164.
18 1837 *Hobart Town Almanack*, p. 93.
19 Quoted in *Mercury*, 14 February 1936.
20 Quoted in W. Denison, *Varieties of Vice-regal Life*, pp. 236–7.
21 *BPP*, vol. 45, 1862, p. 81.

Chapter 7   Punishment

1 1837 *Hobart Town Almanack*, pp. 102–3.
2 Frederick Mackie, *Traveller Under Concern*, p. 162.
3 William Derrincourt, *Old Convict Days*, p. 45.
4 John Sweatman, Journal of a Voyage in the 'Bramble', vol. 2, pp. 323–4.
5 Robert Crooke, *The Convict*, p. 108.
6 *BPP*, vol. 17, 1841, p. 137.
7 Clark Letterbook; G. C. Mundy, *Our Antipodes*, p. 228.
8 Henry Mayhew, *The Criminal Prisons of London*, pp. 303–04.
9 *THAJ*, vol. 22, 1871, p. 111.
10 Mackie, op. cit., p. 161.
11 J. N. Propsting, Personal Recollections of Five Years at Port Arthur.
12 *BPP*, vol. 17, op. cit., p. 126.
13 *THAJ*, vol. 22, op. cit., p. 15.
14 Davis, *The Tasmanian Gallows*, pp. 13–15.
15 Quoted in James Morris, *Heaven's Command*, p. 454.
16 1837 *Hobart Town Almanack*, op. cit., p. 102.
17 Richard P. Davis, *The Tasmanian Gallows*, p. 55.
18 *Hobart Town Courier*, 4 June 1841.
19 ibid., 28 January 1843.
20 Davis, op. cit., pp. 55–6.

Chapter 8   The Separate Prison and the Penitentiary

1 *BPP*, vol. 43, 1849, p. 119.
2 ibid.
3 ibid., p. 195.
4 Quoted in Henry Mayhew, *The Criminal Prisons of London*, p. 102.
5 *BPP*, Report, vol. 28, 1844, p. 5.
6 Mayhew, op. cit., pp. 102–03.
7 *THAJ*, vol. 22, 1871, p. 12.
8 *BPP*, vol. 82, 1853, p. 12.

9 *Mercury*, 18 February 1877.
10 *BPP*, 'Rules and Regulations for the New Separate Prison at Port Arthur', vol. 82, op. cit., pp. 26–33.
11 Quoted in Mayhew, op. cit., p. 142.
12 *Argus*, 12 July 1873.
13 *BPP*, vol. 39, 1855, p. 42; *BPP*, vol. 14, 1857, p. 166.
14 Mark Jeffrey, *A Burglar's Life*, Introduction, p. xii.
15 *Tas. Leg. Co. J.*, vol. 9, 1863, p. 31; *THAJ*, vol. 22, 1871, p. 12.
16 *BPP*, vol. 45, 1851, p. 100.
17 *BPP*, vol. 39, 1855, pp. 41–2.
18 Anthony Trollope, *Australia*, p. 512.
19 *BPP*, vol. 45, 1860, p. 110.
20 CON 35/1; CSD1/79/2157.
21 *BPP*, vol. 39, op. cit., 1855, p. 26; vol. 14, op. cit., 1857, p. 162.
22 ibid., vol. 14, p. 163.
23 George Whittington, Diary of Official Duties.
24 CON 11.
25 *THAJ*, vol. 29, 1875.
26 ibid.
27 *BPP*, vol. 48, 1847, pp. 119–21.
28 *BPP*, vol. 11, 1847–8, p. 92; ibid., vol. 43, 1849, p. 129.
29 *BPP*, vol. 39, 1855, pp. 25 and 40.
30 *BPP*, vol. 14, 1857, p. 161.
31 *Mercury*, 24 March 1870 and 18 February 1877; Commandant's Report for 1857, *BPP*, 1859.
32 *BPP*, vol. 14, op. cit., p. 162; Commandant's Report, op. cit.
33 *Argus*, op. cit.
34 *Mercury*, 7 October 1869.
35 Commandant's Report, op. cit.; CON 11.
36 *BPP*, vol. 14, op. cit., p. 170.

Chapter 9   Timber, Ships and Things

1 Frederick Mackie, *Traveller Under Concern*, p. 168.
2 [Port Arthur Papers], *THAJ*, 1863; *Mercury*, 24 March 1870.
3 *THAJ*, vol. 22, 1871.
4 David Burn, 'Excursion to Port Arthur', p. 287.
5 *Statistical Returns of Van Diemen's Land*.
6 ibid.; J. Bastock, *Australia's Ships of War*, p. 17.
7 C. O. Booth, Journal, December 1837.
8 ibid., February 1838.
9 *Statistical Returns*, op. cit.; *BPP*, vol. 14, 1857, p. 164.

10 CO714/149/1048; *BPP*, vol. 48, 1847, p. 119.
11 Andrew Bell, 'Why Port Arthur Crumbled', *Ecos*, no. 27, 27 February 1981, p. 32.
12 L. J. Blake, *Letters of Charles Joseph La Trobe*, p. 5.
13 *BPP*, HL, vol. 11, 1847–48, p. 68.
14 H. Phibbs Fry, *A System of Penal Discipline*, p. 171.
15 *T. Leg. Co. J.*, vol. 9, 1863, pp. 33–4.
16 G. C. Mundy, *Our Antipodes*, p. 229.
17 *Paris Universal Exhibition 1855*.
18 *THAJ*, vol. 15, 1867, pp. 8–24.
19 *Tasmanian Contributions to the Intercolonial Exhibition, Melbourne, 1875....*
20 George Gruncell, Reminiscences of Port Arthur and Tasman's Peninsula; [Port Arthur Papers], op. cit., *THAJ*, 1874, p. 10; *Mercury*, 30 January 1875.
21 *Tas. Leg. Co. J.*, vol. 9, op. cit., pp. 30 and 32; *THAJ*, vol. 22, op. cit., p. 14; *THAJ*, vol. 25, 1873, p. 9.
22 John Evenden, Experiences of an Officer in the Convict Department, p. 61.
23 *Advertiser*, 23 August 1860; *Mercury*, 31 December 1860.
24 *THAJ*, vol. 22, op. cit., p. 15.
25 *BPP*, vol. 39, 1855, p. 41.
26 *BPP*, vol. 39, 1863, p. 65.
27 *T. Leg. Co. J.*, vol. 9, op. cit., p. 19.
28 [Port Arthur Papers], op. cit., *THAJ*, 1863.
29 *T. Leg. Co. J.*, vol. 6, 1861–2, p. 4.
30 *BPP*, vol. 40, 1861, pp. 56–7.

Chapter 10   Escapes by Land and Sea

1 Owen Stanley quoted in Adelaide Lubbock, *Owen Stanley R. N., Captain of the Rattlesnake*, p. 137.
2 *BPP*, vol. 39, 1855, p. 38.
3 ibid.
4 *Tasmanian Mail*, 23 November 1927.
5 Martin Cash, *The Bushranger of Van Diemen's Land*, 5th ed., pp. 65–6 and 175–8: J. E. Hiener, 'Martin Cash: The Legend and the Man', pp. 71–6 and 81–2; *Australian Dictionary of Biography*, vol. 1, pp. 214–15.
6 *BPP*, vol. 45, 1851, p. 68.
7 *BPP*, vol. 39, 1855, p. 38; vol. 45, 1862, p. 79; vol. 39, 1863, p. 69; *THAJ*, vol. 25, 1873, p. 3.

8 John Evenden, Experiences of an Officer in the Convict Department, pp. 47 and 50–1.

9 CSO5/177/4228.

10 Hobart Town Courier, 28 June 1839; Ian Brand, Escape from Port Arthur, pp. 47–51 and 55.

11 T. Leg. Co. J., vol. 4, 1877, p. 1.

Chapter 11   The Quick and the Dead

1 P. R. Eldershaw, Guide to the Public Records of Tasmania, part 3, pp. 13–14.

2 BPP, vol. 45, 1862, p. 29.

3 T. Leg. Co. J., vol. 6, 1861–2.

4 CSO5/23/449.

5 BPP, vol. 45, op. cit., p. 94.

6 Joan C. Brown, 'Poverty Is Not a Crime', pp. 53 and 173–5.

7 BPP, vol. 45, op. cit., p. 95.

8 THAJ, vol. 3, 1858.

9 CON 31/7 and 37/10.

10 Mark Jeffrey, A Burglar's Life, notes, pp. 189–90.

11 1857 Commandant's Report, BPP, 1859; [Port Arthur Papers], THAJ, paper 100, 1863.

12 Advertiser, 22 August 1860; T. Leg. Co. J., vol. 9, 1863, p. 40.

13 Argus, 12 July 1873.

14 CSD10/22/326; T. Leg. Co. J., vol. 4, paper 48, 1877; THAJ, vol. 22, 1871, p. 83.

15 BPP, vol. 40, 1861, p. 58.

16 BPP, vol. 45, op. cit., p. 95.

17 THAJ, vol. 25, 1873, p. 21.

18 Mercury, 25 November 1867.

19 T. Leg. Co. J., vol. 9, op. cit., pp. 31 and 32.

20 THAJ, vol. 25, op. cit., pp. 20–1.

21 CON 37/4; Argus, op. cit.

22 THAJ, vol. 29, paper 49, 1875.

23 Mercury, 28 December 1860.

24 [John Manton], The Isle of the Dead, p. 4.

25 Hobart Town Courier, 8 April 1836.

26 J. N. B. Plomley (ed.), Friendly Mission, pp. 17 and 785.

27 CON 18/6 and 31/7.

28 CON 37/8.

29 Jeffrey, op. cit., p. 169; J. E. Partington, Random Rot, p. 168.

30 Jeffrey, ibid, n. 16, p. 182.

31 ibid., n. 8, pp. 192–3.

32 ibid., pp. xiv–xv.

33 Advertiser, 23 August 1860.

34 Quoted in Richard Lord, Inscriptions in Stone, p. 14.

35 Advertiser, 22 August 1860.

Chapter 12   The Curtain Falls

1 THAJ, vol. 22, 1871, p. 1; [Port Arthur Papers], THAJ, paper 77, 1873; THAJ, vol. 25, 1873, p. 4.

2 THAJ, vol. 22, op. cit., p. 84.

3 CSD10/48/996; Mercury, 13, 18 and 20 April 1877.

4 Mercury, ibid.

5 CSD10/46/946; CSD10/48/996.

6 CSD10/48/996.

7 ibid.

Chapter 13   A New Act

1 Tasmanian Mail, 22 December 1877.

2 Hobart Gazette, 23 July and 13 August 1889.

3 CSD13/23/257.

4 J. E. Partington, Random Rot, pp. 161–2.

5 CSD13/23/257.

6 Mercury, 7 March 1884.

7 ibid., 31 January 1895.

8 ibid., 4 January 1898.

Select Bibliography

Unpublished papers

Booth, Charles O'Hara, Journal, Archives Office of Tasmania.
——, Instructions for Semaphore, RS31/1, University of Tasmania Archives.
Boyes, G. T. W. B., Extracts from Journal, University of Tasmania Archives.
Brownell, Dr Thomas, Diary Transcript, Archives Office of Tasmania.
Clark, Alexander, Letterbook, RS7/127, University of Tasmania Archives.
Evenden, John, Experiences of an Officer in the Convict Department, RS23/5(2), University of Tasmania Archives.
Gruncell, George, Reminiscences of Port Arthur and Tasman Peninsula, 1889, Archives Office of Tasmania.
Holdsworth, Mrs F., Colonel William Thomas Napier Champ, unpublished lecture to Geelong Historical Society, 1961.
Lempriere, T. J., Diary at Port Arthur, Mitchell Library.
Propsting, J. N., Personal Recollections of Five Years at Port Arthur, Crowther Collection, State Library of Tasmania.
Sweatman, John, Journal of a Voyage in the 'Bramble', vol. 2, A1725, Mitchell Library.
Whittington, George, Diary of Official Duties . . . as Station Officer at Port Arthur, January 1871–June 1872, Mitchell Library.

Books by convicts (except for W. Gates, all men were at Port Arthur)

Cash, Martin, The Bushranger of Van Diemen's Land, 5th ed., Walch, Hobart, 1929 (first published 1870). Cash was illiterate and the book was the work of James Lester Burke, an ex-convict. The book was first called The Adventures of Martin Cash.
Derrincourt, William, Old Convict Days, Penguin, Vic., 1975 (first published 1899). Edited by Louis Becke.
Frost, John, The Horrors of Convict Life, Sullivan's Cove, Hobart, 1973. Two lectures delivered by Frost in England in 1856.

Gates, William, Recollections of Life in Van Diemen's Land, Review Publications, Dubbo, N.S.W., 1977 (first published 1850 and reprinted 1961 by George Mackaness).
Jeffrey, Mark, A Burglar's Life, ed. W. and J. E. Hiener, Angus and Robertson, 1968 (first published 1893). Possibly written by James Lester Burke and edited by Henry Button, the publisher. The editors provide an introduction and notes.
Miller, Linus, Notes of an Exile to Van Diemen's Land, New York, 1846. A Canadian exile, who left the colony in 1846.
Mortlock, John, Experiences of a Convict, ed. G. A. Wilkes and A. G. Mitchell, Sydney University Press, 1965 (first published 1864–5). Contains an introduction and notes.

Books and periodicals

Ackermann, Jessie A., The World Through a Woman's Eyes, Chicago, 1896.
Backhouse, James, A Narrative of a Visit to the Australian Colonies, London, 1843.
Backhouse, James and Tylor, Charles (eds), The Life and Labours of George Washington Walker, London, 1862.
Bell, Andrew, 'Why Port Arthur Crumbled', Ecos, no. 27, 27 February 1981, p. 32.
Blake, L. J., Letters of C. J. La Trobe, Government of Victoria, Melbourne, 1975.
'Bobbin, Tim', Revelations of P[ort] A[rthur], Hobart, 1868.
Brand, Ian, Escape from Port Arthur, Jason Publications, Hobart. (n.d.).
Brown, Joan C., 'Poverty Is not a Crime', Tasmanian Historical Research Association, Hobart, 1972.
Burn, David, 'Excursion to Port Arthur', The Tasmanian Journal of Natural Science, vol. 1, no. 4, Hobart, 1842, pp. 265–95.
Cockburn, Francis J., Letters from the Southern Hemisphere, Calcutta, 1856.
Crooke, Robert, The Convict. A Fragment of History, University of Tasmania Library, Hobart, 1958.

Davis, Richard P., *The Tasmanian Gallows*, Cat and Fiddle Press, Hobart, 1974.

Denison, Sir William, *Varieties of Vice-regal Life*, London, 1870.

du Cane, Sir Charles, *Tasmania—Past and Present*, Colchester, Eng., 1877.

Eldershaw, P. R., *Guide to the Public Records of Tasmania*, part 3 (Convict Department), State Library of Tasmania, Hobart, 1965.

Fry, H. Phibbs, *A System of Penal Discipline*, London, 1850.

Griffiths, Arthur, *Secrets of the Prison-house*, 2 vols, London, 1894.

Hiener, J. E., 'Martin Cash: The Legend and the Man', *Tasmanian Historical Research Association*, vol. 14, 1967, pp. 65–85.

Hobart Town Almanack, Hobart, 1837.

Lempriere, T. J., *The Penal Settlements of Van Diemen's Land*, Royal Society of Tasmania, Launceston, 1954.

Lord, Richard, *Inscriptions in Stone*, Hobart, Lord, 1976.

Lubbock, Adelaide, *Owen Stanley, R.N., Captain of the Rattlesnake*, Heinemann, Melbourne, 1967.

Mackie, Frederick, *Traveller Under Concern*, ed. Mary Nicholls, University of Tasmania, Hobart, 1973.

Mackaness, George (ed.), *Some Private Correspondence of Sir John and Lady Jane Franklin*, 2 vols, Review Publications, Dubbo, N.S.W. (first published 1947).

[Manton, John], *The Isle of the Dead*, London, (n.d., c. 1845).

Masters, W. E., *The Semaphore Telegraph System of Van Diemen's Land*, Cat and Fiddle Press, Hobart, 1973.

Mayhew, Henry, *The Criminal Prisons of London*, Cass, London, 1968 (first published 1862).

[Melville, Harden, S.], *Adventures of a Griffin*, London, 1867.

Melville, Henry, *The Present State of Australia*, London, 1851.

Morris, James, *Heaven's Command*, Penguin, Harmondsworth, 1979.

Mundy, G. C., *Our Antipodes*, 4th ed., London, 1857.

Partington, James E., *Random Rot*, Altrincham, Eng., 1883.

Plomley, N. J. B. (ed.), *Friendly Mission*, Tasmanian Historical Research Association, Hobart, 1966.

[Port Arthur Papers], Archives Office of Tasmania. A bound volume of parliamentary papers.

Reynolds, R., ' "That Hated Stain": The Aftermath of Transportation in Tasmania', *Historical Studies*, vol. 14, 1969, pp. 19–31.

Robertson, Graeme E., *Early Buildings of Southern Tasmania*, 2 vols, Georgian House, Melbourne, 1970.

Robson, L. L., *The Convict Settlers of Australia*, Melbourne University Press, 1976.

Shaw, A. G. L., *Convicts and the Colonies*, Melbourne University Press, 1977.

Stoney, H. Butler, *A Year in Tasmania*, Hobart, 1854.

Trollope, Anthony, *Australia*, University of Queensland Press, Brisbane, 1967 (first published 1873).

Weidenhofer, Margaret, *The Convict Years*, Lansdowne, Melbourne, 1973.

Weidenhofer, Margaret, *Maria Island: A Tasmanian Eden*, Darlington Press, Melbourne, 1977.

West, John, *The History of Tasmania*, ed. A. G. L. Shaw, Angus and Robertson, 1971 (first published 1852).

White, Henry, *Crime and Criminals*, Ballarat, 1890.

Sources of Illustrations

Allport Library and Museum of Fine Arts, State Library of Tasmania 45, 56, 66, 61 bottom right, 62, 63; Archives Office of Tasmania 9, 12, 19, 21, 24, 36 top, 50 top right, 50 bottom right, 61 top right, 66, 73 bottom, 97 right, 102, 122, 123, 124; Beattie Collection, Queen Victoria Museum and Art Gallery vii, 31, 59, 80, 82; Crowther Library, State Library of Tasmania 61 left; Dixson Library, State Library of New South Wales 50 left, 93; Miss P. Finn 55; Mrs F. Holdsworth 74; La Trobe Library, State Library of Victoria v, 4, 11 right, 14, 18 top, 26, 28, 91, 107, 119, 127 top left, 129 left, 129 right; Mitchell Library, State Library of New South Wales 42, 108, 109, 120, 126; National Library of Australia 11 left, 31, 47, 77, 89; Public Record Office, London 13; Queen Victoria Museum and Art Gallery 20, 71, 99 middle, 104; State Library of Tasmania endpapers, 69; State Library of Victoria 44, 70, 76, 78, 79, 81, 92, 95 bottom, 99 right; Tasmanian Museum and Art Gallery jacket, ii, 7, 30 right, 32 bottom, 36, 40, 48, 49, 51, 53, 73 top, 100, 114, 117, 127 bottom right; The *Mercury*, Hobart 127 bottom left; University of Tasmania Archives 30 left, 38 bottom, 32; Maggie Weidenhofer vi, viii, x, 5, 18 bottom, 37, 64 top, 64 bottom, 83 top left, 83 bottom right, 84 top left, 84 bottom left, 84 right, 95, 99 left, 101 top, 102 left, 113, 115, 130, 131.

Index